Latin American Theology

Latin American Theology

Roots and Branches

Maria Clara L. Bingemer

ORBIS BOOKS
Maryknoll, New York 10545

ORBIS BOOKS
Maryknoll, New York 10545

Fathers and Brothers
MARYKNOLL™
TOGETHER IN GOD'S MISSION OF MERCY

Founded in 1970, Orbis Books endeavors to publish works that enlighten the mind, nourish the spirit, and challenge the conscience. The publishing arm of the Maryknoll Fathers and Brothers, Orbis seeks to explore the global dimensions of the Christian faith and mission, to invite dialogue with diverse cultures and religious traditions, and to serve the cause of reconciliation and peace. The books published reflect the views of their authors and do not represent the official position of the Maryknoll Society. To learn more about Maryknoll and Orbis Books, please visit our website at www.maryknollsociety.org.

Copyright © 2016 by Maria Clara Bingemer.

Published by Orbis Books, Box 302, Maryknoll, NY 10545-0302.

Manufactured in the United States of America
Manuscript editing and typesetting by Joan Weber Laflamme.

Library of Congress Cataloging-in-Publication Data

Names: Bingemer, Maria Clara Lucchetti, author.
Title: Latin American theology : roots and branches / by Maria
    Clara L. Bingemer.
Description: Maryknoll, NY : Orbis Books, 2016. | Includes bibliographical references and index.
Identifiers: LCCN 2015045868 (print) | LCCN 2015047774 (ebook) |
    ISBN 9781626981843 (pbk.) | ISBN 9781608336517 (ebook)
Subjects: LCSH: Liberation theology—Latin America. | Theology,
    Doctrinal—Latin America. | Church and social problems—Latin
    America. |
    Catholic Church—Latin America. | Latin America—Church history.
Classification: LCC BT83.57 .B55 2016 (print) | LCC BT83.57
    (ebook) | DDC
    230.098—dc23
LC record available at http://lccn.loc.gov/2015045868

Contents

Series Foreword

Duffy Lectures in Global Christianity

CATHERINE CORNILLE

Never, in the history of Christianity, has Christian faith been expressed in so many forms. While long a global religion, it is only in the course of the twentieth century that the church came to valorize and celebrate the particularity of the different cultures and that local churches were creatively encouraged to engage and appropriate indigenous symbols, categories, and modes of celebration. A milestone in the Catholic Church was the 1975 apostolic exhortation *Evangelii nuntiandi,* which states:

> The individual Churches, intimately built up not only of people but also of aspirations, of riches and limitations, of ways of praying, of loving, of looking at life and the world, which distinguish this or that human gathering, have the task of assimilating the essence of the Gospel message and of transposing it, without the slightest betrayal of its essential truth, into the language that these particular people understand, then of proclaiming it in this language. (no. 63)

The term *language* is here understood in the broad anthropological and cultural sense to touch upon not only translation of the gospel message, but also "liturgical expression . . . catechesis, theological formulation, secondary ecclesial structures, and ministries" (no. 63). It thus involves a thorough rethinking of the gospel in terms and structures resonant with particular cultures, and a focus on the social, political, and spiritual questions and challenges alive in those cultures.

The notions of inculturation and contextualization have since become firmly engrained in Christian theological thinking. One has come to speak of Latino/a theology, African theology, Indian theology, and so forth, each giving way to even more local or focused theologies, such as Igbo theology, Mestizo theology, or Dalit theology. This raises questions about the relationship among all of these forms of theologizing and about the relationship between the individual and the universal church.

The goal of inculturation and indigenous theologies in the first place is, of course, to better serve the local churches and to respond to their particular needs and questions. But many of the cultural riches mined in the process of inculturation may also become a source of inspiration for other churches or for what is called the universal church. *Evangelii nuntiandi* clearly warns, "Let us be very careful not to conceive of the universal Church as the sum, or, if one can say so, the more or less anomalous federation of essentially different churches" (no. 62). It implores individual churches to remain in communion with the universal church. But it does not yet fully appreciate the opportunity for the universal church to learn from local churches. There is still an often unspoken assumption that theological models and currents that have developed in Europe remain normative and that local theologies are but various forms of expression of the same theological insights. However, all theology (including Western theology) entails both universal and culturally particular dimensions, and each attempt to express the gospel within a particular culture may bring out new dimensions of its message relevant for all believers. As the center of gravity of the church is shifting, and as the distinction between local and universal or global is becoming more blurred, it is becoming more than ever important and possible for different theological traditions to engage and enrich one another.

This is why the department of theology at Boston College established the Duffy Chair in Global Christianity. Each year a theologian from a different continent is invited to deliver a series of lectures dealing with the theological challenges and insights arising from his or her particular context. These challenges and insights may focus on ethical questions, theological developments, biblical hermeneutics, spiritual and ritual practices, and so on. The goal is not only to inform faculty and students of the ways in which theology is done in particular parts of the world, but also to raise new questions and offer new insights that might enrich local theological reflection in North America and beyond. The department is very pleased to partner with Orbis Books in order to make the fruit of this theological reflection more broadly available.

The Duffy Chair in Global Christianity was named after Father Stephen J. Duffy (1931–2007), who taught systematic theology at Loyola University in New Orleans from 1971 to 2007, and who was himself deeply engaged with questions of religious and cultural diversity and eager to address these questions in a creative and constructive way. What he wrote about the relationship of Christianity to other religions applies all the more to its relationship to different cultures:

To the extent that Christianity opens itself to other traditions, it will become different. Not that it will be less Christian or cease to be Christian altogether. It will simply be taking one more step toward catholicity, the fullness it claims to anticipate in the coming reign of God.

Introduction

From *Intellectus Fidei* to *Intellectus Amoris*

Why another book about Latin American theology? The answer is very simple. Things have changed radically in the Vatican since Francis became pope. The Latin American pope turned the world's eyes again to the church and the theology of his continent. "Something akin to a resurrection is taking place in the Catholic Church in Latin America, thanks to Pope Francis."[1]

In this revival one of the most important things is the new credibility given to the theology born in Latin America. Theologians who had been punished and forbidden to teach are returning to the universities where their publications are again in bookstores, being studied and discussed. People who asked naively, "Is liberation theology dead?" now see clearly that it is not.

All this points to the timeliness of new reflection on the whole process that this theology has lived and endured. It is time to try to understand the deep obstacles the liberation theologians have endured and overcome and to appreciate better the new face they are presenting to the world.

---

[1] Gerard O´Connell, "Latin American Revival," *America* magazine (June 8–15, 2015).

1

That is the purpose of this book, which has its origins in the Duffy Lectures given at Boston College at the invitation of Catherine Cornille, head of the Department of Theology. Having lived and studied theology, beginning shortly after Vatican II, I was able to perceive firsthand the unfolding of this theology in my country and continent and was able to reflect deeply on this process. To revisit this entire history has been a good experience. Even better was the opportunity to share it with colleagues and graduate students at a privileged forum: Boston College and its Department of Theology.

Following the advice of some colleagues, I am happy to present these reflections in a book format, hoping to help establish a solid citizenship for Latin American theology among North American academics. The book tries to rescue first the history and then work with the contents that emerged from the grassroots, eventually resulting in countless workshops, articles, and books.

The historical roots of liberation theology extend far beyond the era of Vatican II and its immediate aftermath. Those roots are in the prophetic tradition of evangelists and missionaries from the earliest colonial days in Latin America who questioned the type of presence adopted by the church and the way indigenous peoples, blacks, mestizos, and the poor rural and urban masses were treated. The names of Bartolomé de Las Casas, Antonio de Montesinos, Francisco de Vitoria, Antonio Vieira, Frei Caneca, and others can stand for a whole host of religious personalities who have graced every century of the short history of our continent. They are the source of the type of social and ecclesial understanding that emerged in the years after the council—the decades of the 1970s and 1980s—and that are reemerging today with new force and vigor.[2]

---

[2] Leonardo Boff and Clodovis Boff, "A Concise History of Liberation Theology," in *Introducing Liberation Theology* (Maryknoll, NY: Orbis Books, 1987), 66–77.

The first theological reflections that were to lead to liberation theology had their origins in a context of dialogue between a church and a society in ferment, between Christian faith and the longings for transformation and liberation arising from the people.[3] The Second Vatican Council produced a theological atmosphere characterized by great freedom and creativity. This gave Latin American theologians the courage to think for themselves about pastoral problems affecting their countries. This process could be seen at work among both Catholic and Protestant thinkers, with the group Church and Society in Latin America (ISAL) taking a prominent part. There were frequent meetings between Catholic theologians (Gustavo Gutiérrez, Segundo Galilea, Juan Luis Segundo, Lucio Gera, and others) and Protestant theologians (including Emilio Castro, Julio de Santa Ana, Rubem Alves, and José Míguez Bonino), leading to intensified reflection on the relationship between faith and poverty, the gospel and social justice, and the like. In Brazil, between 1959 and 1964, the Catholic Left produced a series of basic texts on the need for a Christian idea of history linked to popular action, with a methodology that foreshadowed that of liberation theology; it urged personal engagement in the world, backed up by studies from the social sciences and illustrated by the universal principles of Christianity.

At a meeting of Latin American theologians held in Petrópolis (Rio de Janeiro) in March 1964, Gustavo Gutiérrez described theology as "critical reflection on praxis." This line of thought was further developed at meetings in Havana, Bogotá, and Cuernavaca in June and July of 1965. Many other meetings were held as part of the preparatory work for the Conference of the Latin American Bishops Conference (CELAM) at Medellín, Colombia, in 1968; these acted as laboratories for a theology based on pastoral concerns and committed Christian action. Lectures given by Gustavo

---

[3] For the next few paragraphs, see ibid.

Gutiérrez in Montreal in 1967 and at Chimbote in Peru on the poverty of the Third World and the challenge it posed to the development of a pastoral strategy of liberation provided powerful impetus toward a theology of liberation. Its outlines were first put forward at the theological congress entitled Toward a Theology of Liberation at Cartigny, Switzerland, in 1969.

Finally, in December 1971, Gustavo Gutiérrez published his seminal work, *Teología de la liberación.*[4] In May, Hugo Assmann had conducted a symposium, Oppression-Liberation: The Challenge to Christians, in Montevideo, and Leonardo Boff was soon to publish a series of articles under the title *Jesus Cristo Libertador.*[5] The door was opened for the development of a theology from and dealing with the concerns of the periphery—concerns that still present an immense challenge to the evangelizing mission of the church.

But in fact the desire and the struggle to integrate faith and the quest for justice have been present in the heart of this continent since the colonizers first arrived. However, in the quick and sometimes dramatic transformations of the Latin American continent in the twentieth century—including the Cuban Revolution in 1959 and the deep changes in the church initiated by Pope John XXIII's pontificate—there was fertile soil for the appearance of liberation theology.

To take the whole of reality as a sign of the times and a call from God in history; to put theological reflection at the intersection of faith with economics, politics, and the social sciences; to read reality from the point of view of the poor and the victims, the excluded, to whom the God of life reveals Godself in a privileged way; to embrace their cause and their dreams; to strive for the changing of this unjust reality as an essential aspect of the following of Jesus

---

[4] English: Gustavo Gutiérrez, *A Theology of Liberation* (Maryknoll, NY: Orbis Books, 1973, 1988).

[5] English: Leonardo Boff, *Jesus Christ Liberator* (Maryknoll, NY: Orbis Books, 1978).

Christ—those are some elements that configure what we commonly call liberation theology.

The first chapter of the book, "Latin American Theology: From Projection to Source," gives the reader a description of the process that the continent lived from the colonial period up to the middle of the twentieth century, particularly the reception of Vatican II at the Latin American bishop's meetings in Medellín (1968) and Puebla (1979). It also describes the crisis that Latin American theology endured during the pontificate of Pope John Paul II, a crisis that continued under Pope Benedict XVI. The chapter also deals with the internal crisis in the school of liberation theology, which made many of the same theologians modify their positions or even criticize the theology they had themselves created.

In the second chapter the subject is the poor, who are the center and heart of Latin American theology. Through an accurate vision of reality, Latin American theologians, together with bishops, religious, and lay people, turned their attention to the poor and the victims of oppression. They understood that during the previous four centuries they had been working mainly with the elites, and that it was imperative to change that covenant. Now the preferential option had to be for the poor, for those without the necessary means to live, who don't have the minimal resources to overcome their situation and to progress into a more decent life. The foundations of the preferential option for the poor challenged the whole Latin American church and created new instruments of evangelization: biblical studies, new forms of lay ministry, the base communities, among others. This chapter includes statements from some of the most prominent theologians of that time in order to make clearer to the reader what it means to make an option for the poor as an imperative rooted in the gospel.

The focus on socioeconomic and political poverty was not very well accepted by some sectors of the church. Liberation theology was accused of Marxism and encountered strong opposition from elements of the hierarchy as well as the

Vatican's Sacred Congregation for the Doctrine of the Faith. However, that crisis, with the entire negative dimension it carried, had some benefits. The main one was that it helped enlarge the scope of liberation theology. An appreciation for other dimensions of poverty—so-called anthropological poverties—began to attract the attention of Latin American theologians. The third chapter deals with one of these, a particularly important one: the situation of women and the question of gender.

Born within liberation theology, the process of women's liberation began with a new solidarity between women theologians and grassroots women. The former understood themselves as spokespersons for the latter and responsible for recovering their rights. The encounters between female theologians and pastoral agents, in a fertile and revealing progression, demonstrated a collective face of passion and a commitment to struggle for justice, inseparable from the building of the kingdom of God.

The encounters, colloquiums, and congresses among women theologians were repeated at national, continental, and intercontinental levels. Through these meetings the theological-pastoral community of women began to attract attention, to arouse curiosity, and to provoke reactions—favorable and unfavorable; at times full of joy and hope; in other cases more aggressive, ironic, or sarcastic, rejecting the uncomfortable novelty. Ecumenical from the beginning, these encounters helped Latin American women theologians to live out—beyond the covenant with the grassroots women—a fertile interaction between Catholics and Protestants that brought about mutual enrichment and built a solid foundation for the future.

The third chapter describes this process, putting names and faces to the protagonists of this beautiful journey and rescuing the main lines and goals they worked on and the challenges they face in the present. Women are definitively an important subject in the Latin American church and theology, and it is difficult, if not impossible, for anyone today to think about or do theology without attending to their reality.

The fourth chapter explores another very important point. Having demonstrated how liberation theology has enlarged its perspective beyond concern for poverty at the socio-economical-political level in order to address anthropological and cultural poverties, including gender, race, and ethnicity, we now see how its concerns have extended beyond human beings to encompass the whole of creation. Ecological concerns, struggles for the sake of the earth, have come to be seen as inseparable from other struggles for justice and well being. Ecology, sustainability, and concern for the life of the earth and the planet are included in the agenda of liberation theology. The challenge of building a habitable world goes hand in hand with empowering people to become the subjects of their own history.[6]

Here we examine Latin American theological thought on ecology by means of two major figures who served as pioneers in this theme. The first is Leonardo Boff, among the most famous of the liberation theologians, who has been working with that issue for decades now. Boff presents a very organized and rigorously systematized view of the ecological crisis, always connecting it with the more authentic aims of liberation theology: to feed the hungry, to build a more friendly and hospitable world for future generations.

The other figure is female theologian Ivone Gebara. She is undoubtedly the key protagonist of ecofeminism, which makes the link between women and the earth. Ecofeminist thinking states that neither the solution of the environmental crisis nor the problem of women's oppression can be treated as an isolated topic. Ecofeminism reflects on the connections among all things that live, an intuition already

---

[6] Just as this book was nearing completion, Pope Francis published his encyclical *Laudato Si'* on ecology. The papal text contains many elements that Latin American theologians, among other thinkers and authorities, have already raised about this important problem.

present among indigenous peoples, the native cultures who embrace a loving intimacy with the earth and its rhythms. Latin American ecofeminism has steadily denounced the androcentric and patriarchal point of view, which has served to diminish reverence for the earth as "mother" and life giver.

Finally, the fifth chapter addresses a subject that has been present since the early history of the continent, though never receiving the attention it deserves, namely, the question of religious diversity.

Given the triple cultural matrix of Latin American—with its indigenous, European, and African sources—the question of religious diversity is essential to our continent. However, it was only after Vatican II that this theme received wide theological attention. Today it is unthinkable to do theology in Latin America without engaging in a cordial and respectful dialogue with indigenous and African religions; the same is true with the great traditions of West and East.

On that point we can see today liberation theology and the theology of religions entering into a deeper and very fruitful dialogue. Both are enriched by this dialogue; for both, their horizons are enlarged. We will give some examples of that in this chapter.

Today, Latin American theology continues its journey, maintaining the legacy of the 1970s and 1980s as a great treasure, while also opening new pathways to be discovered and explored. The crucial point of its contribution to universal theology is the rejection of the tendency to draw reflection mainly from abstract theories or principles. The concepts are important and have to be dealt with rigorously. But the reflection on faith—and that is what theology is and wants to be—is not merely an intellectual reflection *(intellectus fidei)*, but much more, a reflection on the infinite and immeasurable love of God, who inspires and configures the love that moves the theologian to reflect, investigate, speak, and write in service of the people of God *(intellectus amoris)*.

Liberation theology has always tried to be this *intellectus amoris,* understanding itself as a theology at the service of

God's infinite mercy.[7] Constantly challenged by the facts
and the events of reality, Latin American theology is more
than alive. With the emergence of the so-called epistemologies of the South,[8] theology also began to be produced outside Europe. And Latin American theology, namely liberation
theology—together with its northern siblings black theology
and feminist theology—gave special attention to the different contexts, the hidden, silenced, obscure social locations
where theology is elaborated and bears social and political
fruit.

That means they are not only concerned about the
ecclesial identity of theological reflection, but also its social
relevance, its capacity for decolonizing knowledge itself, attentive not only to understanding of but also to the transformation of reality. Finally, they want to contribute to the
advance of social liberation, to the recognition of dignity and
rights. They want to offer a public theology.

We sincerely hope that this theology can help it to be
better known in latitudes outside the global South, "the
end of the world," as said Pope Francis, bishop of Rome,
who presides over all the churches in charity, on the day
of his election.

---

[7] On the distinction between *intellectus fidei* and *intellectus
amoris,* see Jon Sobrino, *The Principle of Mercy: Taking the Crucified Down from the Cross* (Maryknoll, NY: Orbis Books, 1994),
27–46.

[8] See Boaventura de Sousa Santos and Maria Paula Men-
eses, eds., *Epistemologies of the South: Justice against Epistemi-
cide* (London: Paradigm Publishers, 2014), 240.

1.

From Projection to Source

It is not by chance or for lack of a more interesting expression that in 1492 Columbus reported to their very Christian Majesties, the king and queen of Spain, that his expedition had found a "new world." Perhaps it would have been fitting had the new continent been called Colombia and not America. But it was not so. America is the name bestowed on it by a cartographer who mistakenly credited its discovery to Amerigo Vespucci. From then on, the eyes of old Europe began to look upon the southern part of the world as the new, the unknown, the land of adventure and hope; a place where new things could happen, where new life could be built. This new life was not always compatible with justice, freedom, and happiness, not to mention the gospel values exported to the recently discovered continent, accompanied as they were by the sword and the oppressive force of the colonizers.

In any case, the force of the symbol remains. America—the whole of it, North and South[1]—became the name of the new land, the land where, it was believed, one could go in search of a new future and new opportunities. I begin this

---

[1] Cf. John Paul II, *Ecclesia in America*, nos. 37, 59.

reflection about theology in the southern half of the globe by keeping in mind this perspective of eternal novelty, constantly carved by the Spirit within history.

The Arrival of the Gospel in South America

Since the fifteenth-century arrival of the Europeans in America, plurality and diversity were challenges they had to face. Very quickly, perplexities, obstacles, and resistances involved in the complex clash among peoples, cultures, and religions began to emerge. To this very day the theological and pastoral questions that arose at that time remain a burden on the conscience and development of Latin American Christianity.

Very soon, a number of questions began to emerge:

1. *The link between faith and politics.* The Iberian goal of "expanding the faith and the empire" was present in the colonizing movement in Latin America. It is present today in a theology that questions its colonial patrons and wants to rethink its contents from the perspective of the longstanding struggle for justice.

2. *The link between faith and economics.* This is reflected in the transformation of the new empires of the sixteenth century into the commercial-missionary enterprises of the emerging liberal-capitalist order. This process continues today. The contemporary migration in Latin America from historical churches to Pentecostalism is often accompanied by a "theology of prosperity" that is sharply criticized by Latin American theologians of liberation.[2]

---

[2] See, for instance, the works of Jung Mo Sung, "Economics and Theology: Reflections on the Market, Globalization, and the Kingdom of God," in *Global Capitalism, Liberation Theology, and the Social Sciences*, ed. P. M. Zulehner, A. Tausch, and A. Müller (New York: Nova Science Publishers, 2000).

3. *The association between physical and symbolic violence*, due to the association of the cross and the sword. The connection that united military conquest and spiritual conquest was present in Latin American colonization and evangelization from the beginning. It is still present today; the largest Christian continent of the world is the one marked by the gravest injustices.

4. *The acceptance of extreme forms of exploitation of human workers.* Examples include the *encomienda* system or the African slave trade, presented often as a "way of evangelization and salvation," if not of the bodies, at least of the souls.[3]

5. *The abuse of women,* indigenous and African, as the main process of sustaining and expanding the population, resulting in the Latin-American and Caribbean mestizaje, while also consolidating a deeply rooted machismo in the local cultures.[4]

6. *The consolidation of the conception of evangelization as domination,* which is a preliminary and necessary step toward assuring the efficient assimilation of indigenous and African peoples.[5]

For these reasons, doing theology in the Americas—particularly in South America—is not just a matter of abstract reflection on revelation and faith, disconnected from the context in which the word of God is heard and responded to. It is also a reflection on revelation and faith moving forward through history in a way that is inseparable from considerations of social context, politics, and practice. To

---

[3] José Oscar Beozzo, "Humiliated and Exploited Natives," *Concilium* 232/6 (1990); "Evangelização e Escravidão na Teologia Latino-Americana," in *Raizes da Teologia Latino-Americana,* ed. Pablo Richard (São Paulo: Paulinas, 1987), 83–122.

[4] For a good reflection on this topic, see Gilberto Freire, *Casa Grande e Senzala* (Rio de Janeiro: Record, 1998).

[5] See Bartolomé de Las Casas, *The Only Way* (Mahwah, NJ: Paulist Press, 1992).

use a word Latin American theology likes very much, this theology must be rooted in *reality (realidad)*.[6] That is where our reflection must begin.

From the beginning, the question of justice and injustice was inseparable from the announcement of the gospel and the practice of Christian faith in Latin America. This question was courageously raised during the colonization period by ecclesial voices, such as the Dominican Fray Antonio de Montesinos in his preaching on the Island of Hispaniola (Dominican Republic) in an Advent sermon in 1511. He presented himself as a voice crying out in the desert—this desert being the consciences of his listeners. That is how he pleaded with the colonizers: "These are not men? Don't they have rational souls? Aren't you obliged to love them as yourselves? Don't you understand that? Don't you feel that?"[7]

It is not surprising that liberation theologians and historians, writing five centuries later in the light of present oppression and injustice, have drawn inspiration from figures like Montesinos (Dominican Republic), Bartolomé de las Casas (Chiapas, Mexico), Antonio Valdivieso (Nicaragua), Diego de Medellín (Chile), and so many others.[8]

---

[6] This concept of *realidad* was of great importance to Ignacio Ellacuría. See Michael E. Lee, ed., *Ignacio Ellacuría: Essays on History, Liberation, and Salvation* (Maryknoll, NY: Orbis Books, 2013). For reflections on Ellacuría's views, see Jon Sobrino, "The Crucified People and the Civilization of Poverty," in *No Salvation Outside the Poor* (Maryknoll, NY: Orbis Books, 2008), 1–18.

[7] See H. McKennie Goodpasture, ed., *Cross and Sword: An Eyewitness History of Christianity in Latin America* (Maryknoll, NY: Orbis Books, 1989), 11–12.

[8] An appraisal of Las Casas from the perspective of liberation theology can be found in Gustavo Gutiérrez, *Las Casas: In Search of the Poor of Jesus Christ* (Maryknoll, NY: Orbis Books, 1993). For further texts by Las Casas, see George Sanderlin, ed., *Witness: Writings of Bartolomé de Las Casas* (Maryknoll, NY: Orbis Books, 1992).

Together with this connection between evangelization and injustice, there was another perverse link: the conception of European culture as the only one of value and the native cultures as inferior or unimportant. This can be explained by the evolution of Christianity not only as a religion but also as a matrix for the formation of Western civilization. Here history also shows positive efforts on the part of the church to engage in a different synthesis. One of the most obvious examples is the famous Guarani Republic, where the Jesuits not only passed on the gospel and Christian culture to the indigenous people but also affirmed all the native customs that seemed to them to be compatible with human dignity and with a Christian lifestyle. We can think first and foremost of the native languages, which the Jesuits themselves studied and used as means of catechesis, of native arts, and of native community structures.[9]

Nevertheless, this project endured only as long as it could avoid interference by Spanish or Portuguese colonizers. It is very possible that had the Jesuits not been forced to leave these areas, their experience might have led to a more fruitful engagement with languages and culture. However, this did not happen. This project, which pointed toward the possibility of a globalization that respected cultural particularity, was brutally stopped.

The recently discovered "new world" suffered from an evangelization process not always coherent with the sources of Christian faith. At the beginning of Christianity the process of evangelization was rooted in particular cultures and sought to preach the good news from within the different cultures into which it had penetrated.[10] However, the close relationship between Christian faith and European culture as it developed in the Middle Ages (considered *the* culture

---

[9] See Philip Caraman, *The Lost Paradise: The Jesuit Republic in South America* (New York: Seabury, 1975).

[10] See Acts 17, the example of Paul on the Athenian Areopagus.

that should shape the world) led the church to lose sight of the fundamental link between the gospel and cultural diversity. Instead, it tended to make a straightforward identification between Christianity and Western Christendom. It was in this historically conditioned form that the Christian faith was carried by European populations as they embarked on the colonial enterprise from the sixteenth century onward. Thus, conversion to Christianity came to be identified with adoption of the invading culture and a corresponding rejection of the local native and endogenous values.

Ibero-American colonization—whether Spanish or Portuguese—has left a strong legacy to all the peoples of Latin America. This is why we think of Latin America as one cultural, geopolitical, and economic reality. However, another aspect of this legacy is a Eurocentric mindset that tends to blind Latin Americans to the links that connect them. This harmful inheritance from colonialism often weakens their ability to set proper priorities, to sort out their own problems, and to understand how their self-understanding is now anachronistic, given the strategic role that Latin America in fact plays in the global system.

In the postcolonial period that we are living through, we need to be aware that globalization in its present form, sponsored by financial capitalism and by the interests of a small minority of investors, is having a negative effect on the continent. It is threatening cultural identity, and it is undermining the possibility of justice and respect for human rights.[11]

By recalling the history of the church in Latin America between 1960 and 1990, we may find some indications that will help us in the important political, intellectual, and theological tasks that lie ahead.

----

[11] I. Scherrer-Warren, "Movimentos sociais e pós-colonialismo na América Latina," *Ciências Sociais Unisinos* 46/1 (January/April 2010): 26.

The Church of Vatican II and Latin American Theology

The topics of human rights, human promotion, and poverty emerged emphatically after World War II, especially in the Northern Hemisphere and in international organizations like the United Nations.[12] Within the United Nations, the Food and Agricultural Organization (FAO) was founded in 1945 with the aim of ensuring stable food supplies and nutrition, especially in the poor countries.

Before, poverty and hunger were problems more or less spread everywhere. But today there are serious problems, concentrated in particular parts of the world, to the extent that these regions form, alongside the countries of the capitalist West and the communist East an underdeveloped "Third World," to use the term coined by the French geographer Alfred Sauvy in 1952.[13]

At this point the Third World began emerging simultaneously as both a problem and as a new agent on the international scene.

In 1961, the number of countries participating in the FAO increased, now incorporating Latin America, which began to be an important part of the so-called Third World. By this time the Cuban revolution of 1959 had occurred, marking the beginning of a worldwide anti-imperialist struggle to break the bonds of dependence on first-world countries that were perpetuating the legacy of colonialism in new forms.

In face of this new reality the question of how the church was to be present in such places and evangelize their peoples became very controversial. Since the end of the nineteenth

---

[12] In this section I follow closely Paulo Fernando Carneiro de Andrade, "Opción por los pobres em el magistério. Pensamiento social católico desde el Vaticano II hasta la Conferencia de Aparecida," *Concilium* 361 (2015), 31–41.

[13] See Alfred Sauvy, *L'observateur* (August 14, 1952); and Carneiro de Andrade, "Opción por los pobres em el magistério."

century the church had been conscious of having lost the working classes. Pope Leo XIII's encyclical *Rerum novarum*, published in 1891, was an attempt to repair the breach that had opened up between the church and the poor in the era of the industrial revolution. In the twentieth century this same church turned to the Third World, eager to hear the cries of the poor and to answer their fears and aspirations.[14]

On September 11, 1962, in his opening speech for the beginning of Vatican II, Pope John XXIII surprised both the church and the wider world when he affirmed: "Where the underdeveloped countries are concerned, the Church presents herself as she is. She wishes to be the Church of all, and especially the Church of the poor."

Thanks to the pope's words, the idea of the church of the poor broke through. The council opened new paths, and its reception in Latin America led to a structural critique of an evangelization conducted by and for the elites.

The theology of liberation—a new structural approach to theology as a whole—took as its starting point this question: What does it mean to be a Christian in a continent of poor and oppressed people? At stake was a theology aligned with the pastoral practice of a church that wished to make itself freely poor, that placed itself on the side of the poor, and that committed itself to the processes of liberation from all forms of oppression and marginalization.

In addition, this theology wished to speak the language of the indigenous and native cultures and to validate their traditions, their rituals, and their modes of worship. This theology didn't want to abolish those traditions as simply non-Christian, but rather, to respect them. Moreover, where those traditions and cultures lived together with the

---

[14] Cf. Walburt Buhlmann, *The Coming of the Third Church* (Maryknoll, NY: Orbis Books, 1978). See also a more recent book by the same author, *With Eyes to See: Church and World in the Third Millenium* (Maryknoll, NY: Orbis Books, 1990). For a history of Catholic social teaching, see Donal Dorr, *Option for the Poor and the Earth* (Maryknoll, NY: Orbis Books, 2012).

Christian culture brought by colonial evangelization, the effort had to be made to integrate them as a constitutive part of the process of church discourse and praxis. That would be, as the prominent Brazilian philosopher Henrique de Lima Vaz, SJ, said, our chance, as the Latin American church, to make a step from being a church that only projects and reflects a European church and theology to a church that is a source of a native and original living of the gospel, thus generating a new way of thinking and speaking about God, which is what it means to do theology.[15]

The Reception of the Second Vatican Council

At the Medellín Conference of 1968, at which the Latin American bishops assembled to reflect on the implementation of Vatican II in their continent, the church devised a three-point plan of action. The first point was a new set of priorities, inseparably uniting faith and justice. This was accompanied, second, by a new way of doing theology based on the see-judge-act methodology. And third, there arose a new model of church, starting with local communities at the grassroots and in poor areas gathering around the scriptures and learning to express themselves. This was centered on a "popular" reading of the Bible[16] and marked by a desire to be a church of the poor. These became known as base ecclesial communities.[17] These points were confirmed at

[15] Pe. Henrique de Lima Vaz, "Igreja Reflexo/Igreja Fonte," *Cadernos Brasileiros* 46 (March-April 1968):17–22.

[16] The popular reading of the Bible was devised by the Carmelite Carlos Mesters and consists of three steps: examination of reality (facts of life); gospel enlightenment (examination of the biblical text); and transforming action. See Carlos Mesters, *Defenceless Flower: A New Reading of the Bible* (Maryknoll, NY: Orbis Books, 1989).

[17] See "Conclusions of the Second Conference of the Latin American Episcopate," available on the http://www.celam.org website.

the subsequent meeting of the Latin American bishops at Puebla, Mexico in 1979, including (1) a preferential option for the poor; (2) a theology of liberation; and (3) the base ecclesial communities as a new way of being church.[18] This shift in the Latin American church had the support of many prominent church figures.

For instance, after Vatican II, Fr. Pedro Arrupe was elected superior general of the Society of Jesus, the largest religious congregation of the Catholic Church in the whole world. In May 1968 he held a meeting with the Jesuit major superiors of Latin America in Rio de Janeiro. The final document was a policy statement for the Society in the light of the council, reconfiguring and rethinking its apostolate in every field. We can feel in this document the influence of Medellín's proposals:

> We intend to orient our whole apostolate . . . to participate, as best we can, in the common quest of all peoples (whatever their ideology may be) for a freer, more just, and more peaceful society. We want the Society of Jesus to be actively present in the temporal life of humankind today: having as its sole criterion the gospel message as interpreted by the church, exercising no power in civil society and seeking no political goals, seeking solely to shape the consciences of individuals and communities. . . .
>
> Are we capable of responding to the world's expectations? Are our faith and charity equal to the anxiety-ridden appeals of the world around us? Do we practice self-denial sufficiently, so that God is able to flood us with light and energy? Does personal prayer have its proper place in our life, so that we are united with

---

[18] For the Puebla documents, see John Eagleson and Philip Scharper, eds., *Puebla and Beyond* (Maryknoll, NY: Orbis Books, 1979); they are also available at the http://www.celam.org website.

God in this great human task that cannot succeed without God?[19]

Even if those questions were addressed to religious men, such as the Jesuits, every single Christian could take them as a personal invitation and challenge. Christians living in a continent marked by injustice and oppression, such as Latin America, were challenged to respond in a very special way.

And that was what happened. Inspired by the council, not only Latin American Jesuits, but also other religious men and women, bishops, diocesan priests, and lay people made deep changes in their lives and pastoral work so as to dedicate all their apostolic energies to the liberation and development of the continent's poor people. One could see in the Latin American church in this post-conciliar period a growing commitment in favor of the poor and oppressed. The spiritual life generated by this commitment was ardent and impressive. In addition, many wanted to share with the poor, at least in some measure, the effects of injustice and oppression and to make deep and radical changes in their own lives in order to do so.[20]

A Local Setting: The Starting Point for a Global Project

According to Gustavo Gutiérrez's definition, the theology of liberation is "a critical reflection on praxis."[21] However,

---

[19] Provincials of the Society of Jesus, "The Jesuits in Latin America," in *Liberation Theology: A Documentary History*, ed. Alfred T. Hennelly (Maryknoll, NY: Orbis Books, 1990), 78, 82).

[20] See Jean Yves-Calvez, SJ, *Faith and Justice: The Social Dimension of Evangelization* (St. Louis: Institute of Jesuit Sources, 1991). This book includes Pedro Arrupe's speech to the major superiors.

[21] See Gustavo Gutiérrez, *A Theology of Liberation: History, Politics, and Salvation* (Maryknoll, NY: Orbis Books, 1973).

Gutiérrez also says that liberation theology does not begin simply from a critical analysis of reality. It begins with a mystical experience, a deep encounter with the Lord in the face of someone who is poor.[22] Moreover, Gutiérrez and other theologians who continued and deepened this new way of contemplating Christian revelation and faith followed a particular method in building that system: the method known as see-judge-act. In an unjust and oppressive system there cannot be a theology without a social analysis of reality *(see),* an analysis then confronted with scriptural revelation *(judge).* From these two processes should then emerge a transformative strategy that can guide and inspire the political commitments and stances taken up by Christians *(act).*[23]

This theology—which began from social analysis and a program of social action before it became systematic reflection—couldn't be confined to books and to academic courses. It represented the desire of a whole ecclesial community to change its priorities and walk toward the margins and the marginalized. It had to be handed over to the poor in order to help them create their own process of liberation. The ultimate objective was to contribute, humbly, to the struggles of poor people, to make possible a new society, and to enable the poor to become the real subjects and transformative agents of their own history.

Many Christians were committed to these aspirations. Among them, many religious began creating communities

---

[22] Ibid. See also Gustavo Gutiérrez, *We Drink from Our Own Wells: The Spiritual Journey of a People* (Maryknoll, NY: Orbis Books, 1984).

[23] See Clodovis Boff, *Theology and Praxis: Epistemological Foundations* (Maryknoll, NY: Orbis Books, 1987). On the see-judge-act method, see Frans Wijsen, Peter Henriot, and Rodrigo Mejía, eds., *The Pastoral Circle Revisited: A Critical Quest for Truth and Transformation* (Maryknoll, NY: Orbis Books, 2005).

of "insertion" among the poor.[24] Others were committed to doing a new kind of pastoral theology, which had the poor at its center.[25] Still others applied this option and this theology in institutions where they worked, especially schools and universities.[26] Fr. Peter-Hans Kolvenbach, the successor of Fr. Arrupe in leading the Society of Jesus between 1983 and 2008, had no hesitation in saying, "It was Latin America that opened

---

[24] I am referring here, for example, to Jesuit communities that moved out of institutional settings or comfortable houses to live as and/or with the poor. See Benjamin Gonzalez Buelta, SJ, *Bajar al encuentro de Dios. Vida de oración entre los pobres* (Santander: Sal Terrae, 1988).

[25] See, for example, the work of Chilean Ronaldo Muñoz, including *Nova consciência da Igreja na América Latina* (Petrópolis: Vozes, 1979); Muñoz's major work is *The God of Christians* (Maryknoll, NY: Orbis Books, 1990). See also the many works by Brazilian Leonardo Boff, including *Jesus Christ Liberator: A Critical Christology for Our Time* (Maryknoll, NY: Orbis Books, 1978), and *Ecclesiogenesis: The Base Communities Reinvent the Church*, trans. Robert R. Barr (Maryknoll, NY: Orbis Books, 1986).

[26] See, for instance, Brazilian João Batista Libanio, who taught at the PUC-Rio and since 1982 on the faculty of theology of the Jesuits in Belo Horisonte, Brazil. He works include *Spiritual Discernment and Politics* (Maryknoll, NY: Orbis Books, 1982). Other examples include Jesuit Ignacio Ellacuría, rector of the Catholic University of Central America in San Salvador, murdered with his whole community in 1989. See Michael E. Lee, ed., *Ignacio Ellacuria: Essays on History, Liberation, and Salvation* (Maryknoll, NY: Orbis Books, 2013). Ellacuría was a key figure of liberation theology, together with Jesuit Jon Sobrino, a professor at the same university. Both wrote very important works on Latin American theology, such as their edited volume *Mysterium Liberationis: Fundamental Concepts of Liberation Theology* (Maryknoll, NY: Orbis Books, 1993). See also J. Matthew Ashley, Kevin F. Burke, SJ, and Rodolfo Cardenal, SJ, eds., *A Grammar of Justice: The Legacy of Ignacio Ellacuría* (Maryknoll, NY: Orbis Books, 2014).

the eyes of Jesuits to the preferential love for the poor and to true and integral liberation as the priority perspective for the present-day mission of the Society." And we can add: not only the eyes of the Jesuits, but also the eyes of many Christians in the whole world. The author of the book from which this quotation is taken, a French journalist, rightly comments: "This was the beginning of a new phase in social Catholicism."[27]

Difficulties during the 1980s

The 1970s were very fertile and productive years in the development of Latin American theology. Many initiatives began and steadily advanced. A considerable number of bishops and religious authorities supported the option for the poor and the new theology that gave voice to it. Pope Paul VI had some differences with liberation theology, but he never took any initiatives against it.[28]

Many institutes and faculties of theology had professors who were inspired by liberation theology and taught its contents. Many also attended poor parishes during the weekend or even lived in poor areas, in the slums, sharing the life of the poor people. Others, such as Clodovis Boff, lived one semester in the extreme north of Brazil, the state

---

[27] Charles Antoine, *Le sang des justes. Mgr Romero, les jésuites et l'Amérique Latine* (Paris: DDB, 2000), 12. On the Jesuit martyrs of El Salvador, see Jon Sobrino, et al., *Companions of Jesus: The Jesuit Martyrs of El Salvador* (Maryknoll, NY: Orbis Books, 1990); Robert Lassalle-Klein, *Blood and Ink: Ignacio Ellacuría, Jon Sobrino, and the Jesuit Martyrs of the University of Central America* (Maryknoll, NY: Orbis Books, 2014).

[28] He named many progressive bishops for Latin America during his pontificate, from 1963 to 1978, including Oscar Romero in El Salvador, and Dom Hélder Câmara in Brazil.

of Acre, working with the poor, while spending one semester teaching at the Pontifical University in Rio.[29]

The base ecclesial communities (CEBs) spread all over the continent, especially in Brazil. It was estimated in the 1980s that their numbers reached around eighty thousand; the reason was that they were a simpler and horizontal way of being church, based upon a reading of the Bible in confrontation with social reality in order to produce transformative actions to benefit the poor. They understood themselves as people of God, the model of the church proposed in *Lumen gentium,* Vatican II's dogmatic constitution on the church. In a huge country like Brazil, with not enough clergy to attend the Catholic parishes, these communities were a source of hope, offering a way of cultivating faith and linking it with the people's everyday life. They were usually led by sisters and lay people—mostly women. They gathered in huge meetings every two years, where they were joined by bishops, to pray, reflect, and celebrate together.[30]

Leonardo Boff elaborated on the ecclesiology emerging from these communities in *Ecclesiogenesis: A New Way of Being Church.* He was one of the great stars of this movement, together with Gustavo Gutiérrez.[31] The Jesuits were

[29] He taught at the Pontifical University in Rio until 1983, when he was forbidden to teach theology by Cardinal Eugenio de Araújo Salles because of his book *Feet-on-the-Ground Theology: A Brazilian Journey* (Maryknoll, NY: Orbis Books, 1988); originally published as *Teologia pé no chão* (Petrópolis: Vozes, 1984).

[30] See, for instance, Marcello Azevedo, *Basic Ecclesial Communities in Brazil* (Washington, DC: Georgetown University Press, 1987); Alvaro Barreiro, *Basic Ecclesial Communities* (Maryknoll, NY: Orbis Books, 1982); and Jon Sobrino, *The Truth Church and the Poor* (Maryknoll, NY: Orbis Books, 1984).

[31] Gustavo Gutiérrez now belongs to the Dominican Order. Under pressure from Rome, Leonardo Boff left the Franciscans and the priesthood, though he has continued to write and publish on theology and philosophy.

present corporately as a community and with their think tanks, enabling this theology to become a resource for the whole continent and to be taught by their faculties and educational institutes. However, there were many more committed on various levels. The collection *Teología y Liberación*, published simultaneously in different languages and countries, had a solid group of Jesuits in its list of authors.[32]

In 1978, John Paul II was elected pope. This began a hard period for liberation theologians. The major difficulty for the new pope was that in using the see-judge-act method, many liberation theologians relied on Marxist categories of social analysis. The major book on the methodology of liberation theology, *Theology and Praxis,* was by Clodovis Boff,[33] who used the following steps in doing theology: (1) The socio-analytical mediation (analyzing reality with the instruments of the social sciences); (2) the hermeneutical mediation (biblical and philosophical reflection); and (3) the practical mediation (the translation of theology into a practical plan of action).[34]

The Vatican feared that the socio-analytical mediation promoted class struggle and adopted Marxist dialectical materialism as a privileged perspective for reading and

---

[32] These included João Batista Libanio, Xavier Albó, Bartolomé Meliá, Francisco Taborda, Pedro Trigo, and the most famous of all, Jon Sobrino, who wrote notable books rethinking Christology and ecclesiology from the standpoint of "the victims"—his inclusive expression to denote those who suffer from injustice and violence. See *Jesus the Liberator: A Historical-Theological Reading of Jesus of Nazareth* (Maryknoll, NY: Orbis Books, 1994); *No Salvation Outside the Poor, Spirituality of Liberation: Toward Political Holiness* (Maryknoll, NY: Orbis Books, 1988); and *Christ the Liberator: A View from the Victims* (Maryknoll, NY: Orbis Books, 2001).

[33] Boff, *Theology and Praxis.* Originally Boff's doctoral dissertation, this book explicates an epistemology of liberation.

[34] See also Leonardo and Clodovis Boff, *Introducing Liberation Theology* (Maryknoll, NY: Orbis Books, 1987), 22–41.

interpreting history.[35] The Polish pope, who was deeply engaged in supporting the struggle in Eastern Europe (including the Solidarity movement in Poland[36]), did not view this reference to Marxist doctrine in a positive light. Neither did the curia. The discussion about the legitimacy of using Marxist categories to understand an oppressed and conflictive reality such as Latin America became heated. John Paul II, committed to the defeat of communism in Eastern Europe, could not admit or understand how priests, bishops, nuns, and even laity could use a theology that drew on Marxist categories of analysis or how they could openly and publicly give their support to political systems such as Cuba or the Sandinista revolution in Nicaragua.[37]

---

[35] See See Arthur F. McGovern, *Liberation Theology and Its Critics* (Maryknoll, NY: Orbis Books, 1989). For Gustavo Gutiérrez's response, see "Theology and the Social Sciences," in *The Truth Shall Make You Free* (Maryknoll, NY: Orbis Books, 1990), 53–84.

[36] Solidarity was a Polish trade union founded on September 17, 1980, at the Gdask Shipyard under the leadership of Lech Walesa. It was the first trade union in a Warsaw Pact country that was not controlled by the Communist Party. It successfully challenged the government, leading to the election of a Solidarity-led opposition party in elections in 1989.

[37] About Cuba, see Frei Betto, *Fidel and Religion* (New York: Simon and Schuster, 1987). On Christian support for the Sandinista revolution, see Giulio Girardi, *Faith and Revolution in Nicaragua: Convergence and Contradictions* (Maryknoll, NY: Orbis Books, 1989). One of the notable images from these years was of Pope John Paul II, on arriving in Nicaragua, reprimanding Father Ernesto Cardenal, who was serving in the Sandinista government as minister of culture, He had knelt to receive the papal blessing when the pope spoke to him very angrily, ordering him to straighten out his situation with the church. See also the memoir of Ernesto's brother, Fernando Cardenal, SJ, *Faith and Joy: Memoirs of a Revolutionary Priest* (Maryknoll, NY: Orbis Books, 2015).

The discontent of the Vatican with liberation theology was expressed in two instructions published in 1984 *(Libertatis nuntius)* and 1986 *(Libertatis conscientia)*. The first was very critical; the second was somewhat less so.[38] During this period liberation theology experienced many difficulties with the church hierarchy over its use of a Marxist-oriented analysis. Liberation theologians argued that they used these mediations in the same way that Thomas Aquinas in the Middle Ages had used the pagan philosophy of Aristotle. Nevertheless, this critical point has never been completely resolved.[39] The two instructions argued that using the method implied adopting the vision and the perspective that generated it, and that it was incompatible with Christian faith. They argued that a Christian theology could never adopt a materialistic vision of history and life.

What Rome did not seem to understand was that liberation theology truly intended to build a new way of doing theology, and moreover, wanted to do it inside the church. It was an academic proposal but also a pastoral one. It was meant to take place within the church at the service of the poor to help them overcome their poverty and oppression. The more prominent of its theologians, who had studied abroad for years, rethinking theological topics from the perspective of the poor, obtained degrees and wrote books and articles. However, none of them wanted to walk away from the church. There was no intention of forming a parallel church, or a "popular church," as the Vatican suspected.

---

[38] In 1986, the Boff brothers published an open letter to Cardinal Ratzinger (who would later become Pope Benedict XVI). The text analyzed *Libertatis conscientia,* wherein Ratzinger tried to correct the supposed deviations of liberation theology in Latin America. With lots of irony and a good deal of courage the Boff brothers expressed their disagreement. For another critique of *Libertatis conscientia,* see Juan Luis Segundo, *Theology and the Church: A Response to Cardinal Ratzinger and a Warning to the Whole Church* (New York: Winston Press, 1985).

[39] See McGovern, *Liberation Theology and Its Critics.*

Many of the books produced during this golden age of liberation theology were translated into English, Italian, French, and German, among other languages.[40] Plans for a collection of fifty volumes—Theology and Liberation—were halted after only twenty volumes due to Rome's intervention. Many theologians were reduced to silence, forbidden to teach, or faced many restrictions in doing so. Leonardo Boff was one of them.[41]

Liberation theology resisted these invectives. The most famous theologians—such as Gustavo Gutiérrez and Leonardo Boff, for instance—went to Rome to try to dialogue with the Vatican. The results were not very hopeful. In a parallel movement the policy of John Paul II's pontificate began to change the face of the Latin American episcopate. The newly appointed bishops ran counter to the prophetic and courageous bishops who had previously supported and struggled for the base ecclesial communities, who had adopted the preferential option for the poor, and who supported liberation theologians. Today, that generation is aged or dead and the current generation of bishops has tended to issue from new conservative movements.

In 1989, the world crisis culminating with the fall of the Berlin Wall and of Eastern European state socialism had deep repercussions on the whole of Latin American theology. Many of the lay leaders, who had emerged from the base communities and who were deeply committed to social and political struggle on the basis of their Christian faith, experienced a deep crisis. Some of them lost hope and left the church as well as their religious commitments.

---

[40] Most of them were published in English by Orbis Books, including many of the original volumes, in the series Theology and Liberation.

[41] In 1985 I replaced him, teaching his courses on systematic theology in Petrópolis, a city in the middle of the mountains close to Rio de Janeiro. See Harvey Cox, *The Silencing of Leonardo Boff: The Vatican and the Future of World Christianity* (New York: Meyer Stone, 1988).

Outside the church it looked as if the socialist idea of utopia had been defeated, and the only possible model of society was the capitalist one. Without the balance of power provided by the socialist bloc (the Second World), there was no means for thinking about a way of living other than through the market economy and the neoliberal society. The "end of history" seemed to have arrived.[42] A great sense of disillusionment overcame the hearts and minds of many who had been committed and supportive of the proposals of liberation theology, who had learned to read and interpret the gospel through that model.

In 1991, on the occasion of John Paul II's encyclical *Centesimus annus,* which marked the centenary of the encyclical *Rerum novarum,* Clodovis Boff argued in an excellent article titled "The Militant Church of John Paul II and the Triumphant Capitalism" that while in a democratic world it is legitimate to struggle against an ideology or a social theory, it is unacceptable to deceive the poor of Christ and to defraud their hope.[43] It is notable that the same Clodovis Boff, who was one of the strongest apologists for liberation theology, wrote an article in 2007 that took a markedly critical stance toward liberation theology. He accused it of making the poor the center of theology, which could mean putting them in the place of God. He went on to reaffirm that the only standard for theology is Christ the Lord; everything else, including the poor, is a secondary theme.[44]

Many other Latin American theologians, among them Clodovis's brother Leonardo Boff, answered his essay and

---

[42] See Francis Fukuyama, *The End of History and the Last Man* (New York: Free Press, 1992).

[43] "A Igreja militante de João Paulo II e o capitalismo Triunfante. Reflexões sobre a Centesimus Annus à luz do Terceiro Mundo," in F. Ivern and M. C. Lucchetti Bingemer, *Doutrina Social da Igreja e Teologia da Libertação* (São Paulo: Loyola, 1994), 87–111.

[44] Clodovis Boff, "Teologia da Libertação e volta ao fundamento," *Revista Eclesiástica Brasileira* 67/268 (October 2007): 1001–22.

criticized it strongly.[45] Clodovis Boff then replied to them
with a self-criticism for having previously fallen into the
temptation of magnifying and idealizing the poor.[46] He reaffirmed his conviction that a legitimate liberation theology
has to have a clear awareness that it is merely a partial
theology, avoiding the pretense of offering a comprehensive
theology coextensive with the whole Christian mystery. Liberation theology—says Clodovis Boff—has a particular perspective within the greater perspective of faith. He invokes
Karl Rahner, who, writing in 1984, just before his death,
notes: "Liberation theology is conscious of its limited meaning within the whole of Catholic theology." This theology,
therefore, Clodovis Boff continues, needs to be conscious
of itself as not representing a totally new theology that is in
conflict with the substance of the great theological tradition,
but rather understanding itself as a "new step" in continuity with this same tradition, as John Paul II states in the
instruction *Libertatis conscientia* (nos. 23, 71, 99).

So, after all that, when even one of its most distinguished
protagonists is so sharply critical, should we conclude that
liberation theology is dead?

On the contrary, with historical distance we can now
more fully evaluate that crisis of liberation theology as a
positive one. It forced liberation theologians to expand their
horizons and realize that the process of liberation was not
only about human beings, but also about the whole of creation. Ecological concerns and the struggle to protect the
earth came to be seen as indivisible from human concerns.

---

[45] Leonardo Boff, "Pelos pobres e contra a estreiteza do
método," *Notícias do Dia*, IHU On-Line (May 27, 2008); Luiz
Carlos Susin and Erico Hammes, "A Teologia da Libertação e a
questão de seus fundamentos: em debate com Clodovis Boff,"
Revista Eclesiástica Brasileira 68/270 (2008): 277–99; Francisco de Aquino Junior, "Clodovis Boff e o método da Teologia
da Libertacao. Uma aproximação cítica," *Revista Eclesiástica
Brasileira* 68/271 (2008): 597–613.

[46] Clodovis M. Boff, "Volta ao fundamento: réplica" *Revista
Eclesiástica Brasileira* 68/272 (2008): 892–927.

Christian theology, even in its more open and up-to-date forms, such as liberation theology, has been accused of having an excessively anthropocentric approach to the world and human life. The traditional interpretation of the Genesis mandate to reproduce and dominate the earth was considered responsible for humankind's greedy attitude toward nature and creation. To reverse this idea, theology had to evolve. Christian consciousness grew increasingly aware that one always has to go forward, searching for newer and bigger ways to achieve true liberation according to the tenets of the Bible and the gospel of Christ.

Environmental sustainability and care for the earth came onto the liberation agenda alongside new subjects addressing such wider issues as gender, race, ethnic and religious diversity. New forms of reflection began with the conviction that the struggle for justice also implies building a more sustainable world. Everything that harms human beings is harmful to the planet as well. If the human race continues to destroy nature and life in all its manifestations, very soon human beings will not be able to survive. The inseparable link between the struggle for justice and the struggle for nature and biodiversity has become central to committed theological reflection.[47]

In addition, the emergence of new subjects brought a valid and precious interpellation to liberation theology. Women and the whole question of gender and sexual diversity figured strongly in the reflection of Latin American theologians, in particular when female theologians raised their voices and started to write and publish their own theological reflections. In addition, the issue of race, so important in a continent where slavery was present until the end of the nineteenth century, became ever more pronounced, especially as theologians of African descent began bringing

---

[47] See, for instance, Leonardo Boff's works on ecology and care for the earth: *Ecology and Liberation: A New Paradigm* (Maryknoll, NY: Orbis Books, 1995); *Cry of the Earth, Cry of the Poor* (Maryknoll, NY: Orbis Books, 1997); and others.

their questions and issues to the theological debate. In a continent with so many ethnicities, the debate over ethnicity and the whole indigenous question, which is linked to the questions of ecology and cultural diversity, has proved to be a central one. The reflection on the original peoples *(pueblos originarios)*, especially in Argentina, gave birth to a new theological school: the teología del pueblo (theology of the people), which greatly influenced Cardinal Bergoglio of Buenos Aires (now Pope Francis).

Finally, the plurality of new subjects has brought into relief the need for dialogue with other religious denominations and tradition.

A Theological Source of Many Good and New Things

The legacy of Vatican II, found especially in the pastoral constitution *Gaudium et spes*, calls attention to the duty of being attentive to the human as the heart of the church's vocation and mission. According to the opening words of that document:

> The joys and the hopes, the griefs and the anxieties of the men of this age, especially those who are poor or in any way afflicted, these are the joys and hopes, the griefs and anxieties of the followers of Christ. Indeed, nothing genuinely human fails to raise an echo in their hearts. For theirs is a community composed of men. (no. 1)

The big question of humanity, which God loved to the point of sending the Son, is and must be the main concern of the church and of theology. In addition, among those men and women who make up this humanity, the poor and afflicted of all kinds are always there, their faces calling for justice and recognition. Unfortunately, poverty is far from being overcome, and justice is not a fact in our world, certainly not in Latin America, in spite of all the efforts of the local church. Moreover, in continents like Latin America, where one-third of the population is below the line of extreme poverty, the option for the poor remains a real priority. It is by putting that question at the center of its reflection that Latin American theology—namely, liberation theology—found its vocation and its God-intended purpose. And because of that, it continues to put this question of the poor and justice at the center of its thought. That is the reason we can affirm that it is still alive. There are theologians who continue to read and interpret reality with the same *pathos* and the same *ethos* as in the foundational years. Pedro Trigo, a committed liberation theologian of the first generation, says:

> This is decisive. If it is not there, theological elaboration will be reduced to scholastics, an academic practice which, at best, can be rigorous and full of good intentions, but won't be anything other than a mere intellectual product. It can refer very correctly to reality, but without possessing its density, instead reducing itself to be a mere reference to it.[48]

The conclusion is that liberation theology continues to exist, indeed to remain very much alive, because theologians still exist who live their theology as a second act, according to this pathos and this ethos, which is the primary act. There are still theologians who conceive their theology as a mercy seeking understanding—*intellectus amoris*—which is also a theology of grace and liberation.

According to Jon Sobrino the first awakening for humankind in modern times was the awakening from dogmatic slumber, thanks to Kant, Hegel, and the masters of sus-

---

[48] P. Trigo, "Ha muerto la Teología de la Liberación? La realidad actual y sus causas (II)," *Revista Latinoamericana de Teología* 64 (2005): 291.

picion. Its consequence is the *intellectus fidei*. The second awakening, this time from the slumber of inhumanity, helps us to understand the need for theology to be preferentially *intellectus amoris*. And this is a theology concerned about "taking the crucified peoples down from the cross." Liberation theology has always tried to be this *intellectus amoris*, understanding itself as a theology at the service of God's infinite mercy.[49]

In recent years liberation theology has not given up this calling to be *intellectus amoris*. Now, this intelligence of love is richer than before, for it has enlarged its scope and recognized other anthropological poverties besides the socioeconomic and political kind. It now recognizes, among others, the whole issue of ecology; the injustices of gender, race, and ethnicity; and the need to overcome interreligious prejudice. All these are also anthropological poverties that afflict human beings, and liberation theology continues to give very close attention to all of them.

---

[49] Jon Sobrino, "Awakening from the Sleep of Inhumanity," in *The Principle of Mercy: Taking the Crucified People from the Cross* (Maryknoll, NY: Orbis Books, 1994), 1–11.

2.

The Poor as Subject and as Method

The option for the poor arose explicitly during the second assembly of the Episcopal Conference of Latin America (CELAM), which occurred in Medellín, Colombia, in 1968.[1] This occurred in the context of an effort to apply the teachings of the Second Vatican Council in a continent marked by massive poverty. As Clodovis Boff notes:

> It was not just Vatican II, but together with it, the *concrete circumstances* in which the continent lived, that caused the church in Latin America to redefine its identity. And this redefinition happened as connected with this reality and determined a strongly social perspective. The Church in Latin America was characterized as a "social Church," a prophetic Church, a Church of the poor, a liberating Church.[2]

---

[1] See Gustavo Gutiérrez, *The Power of the Poor in History* (Maryknoll, NY: Orbis Books, 1983), 25–90.

[2] Clodovis Boff, "A originalidade historica de Medellín," available in Portuguese on the http://servicioskoinonia.org website.

This option attempted to direct the addressee as well as the content of evangelization. According to the final document of Medellín:

> The Latin American bishops cannot remain indifferent in the face of the tremendous social injustices existent in Latin America, which keep the majority of our peoples in dismal poverty, which in many cases becomes inhuman wretchedness. A deafening cry pours from the throats of millions of men, asking their pastors for a liberation that reaches them from nowhere else. "Now you are listening to us in silence, but we hear the shout which arises from your suffering," the Pope [Paul VI] told the 'campesinos' in Colombia. ("Poverty of the Church," nos. 1–2)[3]

In section III of the same chapter, called "Pastoral Orientations," the document offers even more concrete and incisive statements and commitments:

> Because of the foregoing we wish the Latin American Church to be the evangelizer of the poor and one with them, a witness to the value of the riches of the Kingdom, and the humble servant of all our people. Its pastors and the other members of the People of God have to correlate their life and words, their attitudes and actions to the demands of the Gospel and the necessities of the men of Latin America. (no. 8)

The subtitle, "Preeminence and Solidarity," points to the roots of what will come to be called a preferential option for the poor:

---

[3] CELAM, "Poverty of the Church" (September 6, 1968). The document is available in English in numerous books and on several websites, including http://www.shc.edu.

The Lord's distinct commandment to "evangelize the poor" ought to bring us to a distribution of resources and apostolic personnel that effectively gives preference to the poorest and most needy sectors and to those segregated for any cause whatsoever, animating and accelerating the initiatives and studies that are already being made with that goal in mind.

We, the bishops, wish to come closer to the poor in sincerity and brotherhood, making ourselves accessible to them.

This has to be concretized in criticism of injustice and oppression, in the struggle against the intolerable situation which a poor person often has to tolerate, in the willingness to dialogue with the groups responsible for that situation in order to make them understand their obligations.

We express our desire to be very close always to those who work in the self-denying apostolate with the poor in order that they will always feel our encouragement and know that we will not listen to parties interested in distorting their work. (nos. 9–11)

In 1979, eleven years after Medellín, the Latin American bishops' next general conference occurred in Puebla, Mexico. The final Puebla document defines more solidly and consistently the preferential option for the poor. The text speaks not about a desideratum for the future, but about something that had been on the move in the continental church for more than a decade.

The objective of our preferential option for the poor is to proclaim Christ the Savior. This will enlighten them about their dignity, help them in their efforts to liberate themselves from all their wants, and lead them to communion with the Father and their fellow human beings through a life lived in evangelical poverty. (no. 1153)[4]

The basis for this option resides in the announcement of the gospel of Jesus (no. 1141) and in the announcement of God's defense of and love for those who suffer due to the mere fact of being poor (no. 1142); historically, it is compelling because of the "scandalous reality of economic imbalances in Latin America" (no. 1154). It is a preferential option but not an exclusive option. Revelation and salvation are universal, and to opt for the poor does not entail neglect for the evangelization of others. Nevertheless, Puebla states that even for the evangelization of those who are not poor this option is important and necessary. "The witness of a poor Church can evangelize the rich whose hearts are attached to wealth, thus converting and freeing them from this bondage and their own egotism" (no. 1156).

The concluding document of the Puebla conference recalls the option for the poor of Medellín, confirming that its novelty and importance go beyond the pastoral dimension. It launches a whole logic and dynamism, which permeates everything, so that it configures the whole being and practice of the church, spiritually and historically. It is more than a temporal option. It is a way of living and acting in this world and of simply being human. It is the only option capable of humanizing history. It requires the church in Latin America to rethink its method of evangelization and its internal life and structures, creating an open exchange between a church that announces the good news to the poor one and one that is, in turn, evangelized by them. While affirming that the option for the poor is rooted in God and in Jesus Christ, the church is challenged to rethink its announcement of who God and Jesus Christ are. It is an

---

[4] An English translation of the final Puebla document can be found in John Eagleson and Philip Scharper, eds., *Puebla and Beyond* (Maryknoll, NY: Orbis Books, 1980).

option for life informed by faith, as God is the God of life, who wants life in its fullness for all creatures.[5] After the Puebla conference CELAM did not convene another assembly until 1992, in Santo Domingo in the Dominican Republic. This was a difficult meeting. By this point the Vatican had set a course in opposition to liberation theology. Those were the years that the great theologian Karl Rahner described as an "ecclesial winter."[6] The preparatory documents for the Santo Domingo conference clearly marked a departure from the priorities set in Medellín and Puebla.

The fourth CELAM conference convened on the Island of La Hispaniola, where Columbus had arrived in 1492. The governing powers of Latin American and many other civil institutions were poised to celebrate the 500th anniversary of the discovery of America. However, there were other institutions and movements—including the more progressive wing of the Latin American church—which opposed such a triumphalistic celebration, as well as the anachronistic terminology of *discovery*. The argument was that Columbus did not discover a continent but instead had arrived in a continent where native populations were living in peace, and that he had inaugurated an era of violent colonization. All these political arguments affected the atmosphere at the Santo Domingo conference.[7] In the end, the final document included a number of positive elements, emphasizing the

---

[5] See Jon Sobrino, "Depth and Urgency of the Option for the Poor," in *No Salvation Outside the Poor* (Maryknoll, NY: Orbis Books, 2008), 19–34.

[6] Karl Rahner, interview by David Seeber, March 5, 1984, Rahner's birthday and some weeks before his death. In this interview, which would be his last, Rahner maturely analyzed the circumstances of the church and used the expression that can be translated into English as "ecclesial winter" to refer to what was happening in the church.

[7] See Alfred T. Hennelly, ed., *Santo Domingo and Beyond* (Maryknoll, NY: Orbis Books, 1993), which includes the documents and a number of commentaries, including a critical assessment by Jon Sobrino.

role of the laity, calling them the protagonists of the new evangelization.[8] Nevertheless, the prophetic winds that blew in Medellín and Puebla seemed weakened and distant.

In 2007, the fifth conference of CELAM held in Aparecida, Brazil, returned the attention of the church to the central importance of ministering to the poor. In the inaugural session, on May 13, Pope Benedict XVI reaffirmed the option for the poor as an evangelical priority. In his own words: "The preferential option for the poor is implicit in the Christological faith in the God who became poor for us, to enrich us with his poverty."

In 2013, Pope Francis further emphasized this undeniable priority in his apostolic exhortation *Evangelii gaudium*:

> For the church, the option for the poor is primarily a theological category rather than a cultural, sociological, political or philosophical one. God shows the poor "his first mercy." This divine preference has consequences for the faith life of all Christians, since we are called to have "this mind . . . which was in Jesus Christ" (Phil 2:5). Inspired by this, the Church has made an option for the poor which is understood as a "special form of primacy in the exercise of Christian charity, to which the whole tradition of the Church bears witness." This option—as Benedict XVI has taught—"is implicit in our Christian faith in a God who became poor for us, so as to enrich us with his poverty." This is why I want a church which is poor and for the poor. They have much to teach us. Not only do they share in the sensus fidei, but in their difficulties they know the suffering Christ. We need to let ourselves be evangelized by them. The new evangelization is an invitation to acknowledge the saving power at work in their lives

---

[8] CELAM, Final document, Fourth Conference of the Latin American Episcopate, Santo Domingo (1992), no. 97.

and to put them at the center of the church's pilgrim way. We are called to find Christ in them, to lend our voice to their causes, but also to be their friends, to listen to them, to speak for them and to embrace the mysterious wisdom, which God wishes to share with us through them. (no. 198)

In order to understand clearly what the church is saying when proposing the poor as a priority and a fundamental option for Christian life and for theology, it is imperative to ask some questions: What does the church mean by *poor*? How can a social reality become a theological category and concept?

Who Are the Poor?

In his groundbreaking work *A Theology of Liberation* (1971), Peruvian theologian Gustavo Gutiérrez clarifies his understanding of the poor and poverty.

First, he writes, "material poverty" is an evil to be opposed and fought. It is not a result of destiny or an occasion to practice charity, but a degrading dynamism that denigrates human dignity and which must be opposed, rejected, and eliminated from the world.

Second, poverty should not be considered as a result of fate or laziness. It is due to structural injustices that privilege the few while marginalizing the many. Most important, Gutiérrez affirms that poverty is not inevitable and unchangeable. Collectively and in solidarity the poor can organize themselves and struggle for social change.

Third, poverty is a complex reality, not limited to its economic dimensions. To be poor is to be insignificant, to be regarded as having no worth to society. One who is poor is constantly vulnerable and exposed to premature death. In the words of a Brazilian poet, João Cabral de Mello Neto, the poor die

From ambush before twenty
From old age before thirty
From hunger a little a day[9]

Jon Sobrino also tries to define what we mean by the poor in Latin American liberation theology. The poor are, very concretely, those human beings for whom the fundamental fact of living is a heavy burden and a hard struggle in the midst of total insecurity and precarious conditions, even concerning the most elementary question of where their next meal will come from.[10] Biblically speaking, the poor are those who are bent, bowed, humiliated, ignored, and despised by society for life.

That is the understanding of the poor in Latin American theology. The poor are those who are first of all socioeconomically poor. Frei Betto, another widely known liberation theologian and writer, uses powerful words to describe this reality in our continent:

To speak about human rights in Latin America is a luxury. Here, we are still struggling for the animal rights, because to eat, to have a roof overhead, are rights enjoyed by livestock. I never saw a calf abandoned in the streets of Brazil or a cow at the corner of the street waiting for someone to give it food. However, there are 8 million abandoned children and thousands of beggars searching for something to eat in garbage cans.[11]

---

[9] João Cabral de Melo Neto, "De emboscada antes dos vinte; de velhice antes dos trinta; de fome um pouco por dia," *Morte e Vida Severina.*

[10] See Sobrino, "Depth and Urgency of the Option for the Poor."

[11] Frei Betto, "Direitos humanos ou direitos animais?" In Portuguese at http://www.correiocidadania.com.br.

Together with this concrete, socioeconomic poverty, there is also a sociocultural poverty. This element was very much stressed by the theology of the people *(teología del pueblo)*, a theology with which the then-archbishop of Buenos Aires, Jorge Mario Bergoglio, today Pope Francis, was very connected. The theology of the people was—according to Gustavo Gutiérrez—a stream within liberation theology with its own characteristics.[12]

According to Juan Carlos Scannone, a prominent representative of this theology, the elements of the theology of the people are as follows:

1. To take as a starting point the aboriginal Latin American peoples *(pueblos originarios)*, whose wisdom and religion is frequently inculturated by the people of God.

2. The preferential use of a historical-cultural analysis as a mediation to interpret and to judge the historical and social reality of the poor in the light of faith.

3. To use human sciences, such as history, cultural anthropology, and the science of religion, in addition to symbols and narratives, in a more synthetic and hermeneutical way, without despising the more analytical sciences.

4. Since the beginning this stream criticized the use of Marxist instruments of analysis by liberation theology, considering them not critical enough. The poor, nevertheless, have a special place within the central categories of the theology of the people: people, popular religion, culture.

Liberation theologians have never denied the importance of cultural poverty. Together with socioeconomic poverty, there is also sociocultural poverty, which is equally hard and heavy. There is racial, ethnic, and sexual oppression and discrimination. In addition, very often, for many women and indigenous people, the difficulty of living increases due to their gender and to the fact of being of African descent.

---

[12] Gutiérrez, *The Power of the Poor in History,* 25.

This additional difficulty is not independent from the socio-economic reality but rather exacerbates it.

The theology of the people remained mostly an Argentinian phenomenon, while the rest of the continent predominantly adhered to the mainstream version known simply as liberation theology. Now, the theology of the people has gained more attention due to the fact that one of its champions, Cardinal Jorge Bergoglio of Buenos Aires, has become pope, and Jesuit Juan Carlos Scannone is his close adviser. Certainly, Fr. Scannone never understood the theology of the people as in opposition to liberation theology. On the contrary, he states it is the Argentinian version of liberation theology. The difference is that the theology of the people never used Marxist categories of analysis, as did liberation theology.[13]

Regardless of the different streams, liberation theology was rooted in a specific methodological discourse: see-judge-act.[14] In addition, this theology was not meant to remain in books and in academic courses, but instead was meant to relate back to the poor and help them put their own process of liberation into action. Liberation theology sought to build a new society by struggling alongside the poor in order to enable them to be the subjects of their own history.[15]

The Church of the Poor: A Concept with Remote Roots

Even if it became more visible and systematically organized in the twentieth century after Vatican II, the preferential option for the poor was not a recent invention; it was one of

---

[13] Fr. Juan Carlo Scannone, interview in *IHU noticias,* available in Portuguese at http://www.ihu.unisinos.br.

[14] This method had been systematized by Catholic Action, a lay movement born in France and very strong in Latin America in the 1950s and the 1960s. It helped Christians who engaged socially in the search for a critical understanding of reality and the commitment with transformative action.

[15] See Leonardo and Clodovis Boff, *Introducing Liberation Theology* (Maryknoll, NY: Orbis Books, 1987).

the basic principles of Catholic social teaching. The fathers of the church had already expressed the central importance of the poor in the first four centuries. For example, Saint Ambrose writes:

> You are not making a gift of your possessions to the poor person. You are handing over to him what is his. For what has been given in common for the use of all, you have arrogated to yourself. The world is given to all, and not only to the rich.[16]

Or Basil the Great, who writes in his "Commentary on Matthew 25:31–46":

> The bread that is left by you is the bread of the hungry. The clothing you keep moldering is the clothing for the naked. The shoes you do not use are the shoes of those who go barefoot. The money you hide is the money of the poor. The works of charity you do not practice are one among many injustices that you commit. Who accumulates more than necessary practices crime.

Also, Saint Gregory of Nyssa writes that "solidarity with the poor is the law of God, not a mere counsel."[17]

This centrality of the poor is so central to the gospel and the tradition of the Christian church that it is even present in the church's Canon Law, which states: "The Christian faithful are obliged to promote social justice and, mindful of the precept of the Lord, to assist the poor from their own resources" (canon 222 §2). This social perspective of Christianity always existed, but began to be organized in the nineteenth century

---

[16] As quoted in *Populorum progressio* (1967), no. 23.

[17] Gregory of Nyssa, "On the Love of the Poor," in Susan R. Holman, "The Hungry Are Dying: Beggars and Bishops in Roman Cappadocia," *Oxford Studies in Historical Theology* (Oxford University Press, 2001), 193–206.

in the context of dialogue with a secularized, industrialized world with Pope Leo XIII's encyclical *Rerum novarum*. What Vatican II did was to call the faithful back to the origins of their faith, to the sources of their salvation, in order to live their faith fully in commitment for justice and charity.

Pope John XXIII, in convening the council, spoke of one of his aims: that the church should recover its true identity as the church of the poor.[18] Many of the council fathers and their theological advisers were very moved by this theme. Some viewed the issue of the poor as a pastoral question to be addressed with a good and well-organized working pastoral strategy, while others—including Latin Americans Dom Hélder Câmara from Brazil and Dom Manuel Larrain from Chile—had another vision. They saw the question of the poor as a structural question. Accordingly, they emphasized that poverty was the fruit of injustice and affirmed the need for the church to accompany the poor in the process of their struggles for liberation.

Cardinal Lercaro of Bologna played an important role. On December 6, 1962, before the general session, he delivered a long speech entitled "Church and Poverty." He would further deepen his reflections on the subject at a conference in Beirut in 1964.[19]

Paulo Fernando Carneiro de Andrade synthesizes Lercaro's position:

- The question of the poor constitutes a mystery founded in the mystery of the Incarnation itself. The kenotic process includes the fact that

---

[18] The phrase "church of the poor" was first used by Pope John XXIII in his inaugural address to the fathers of the Second Vatican Council in 1962.

[19] The texts are cited in Paulo Fernando Carneiro de Andrade, "Opción por los pobres en el magistério. Pensamiento social católico desde el Vaticano II hasta la Conferencia de Aparecida," *Concilium: Revista Internacional de Teología* 361 (June 2015), 31–41.

the Word did not assume just any human flesh (sarx), but poor flesh, and this is not a matter of indifference.

• The poor have a special place in the economy of salvation, in light of the Messianic prophecies of Isaiah; this is clear in the Beatitudes and in Jesus' inaugural Sermon in the synagogue of Nazareth. ("Blessed are the Poor in Spirit," and "I have come to bring Good News to the Poor.")

• Salvation is always in conformity with Christ, poor, crucified and persecuted.[20]

In addition, he offers some christological illuminations:

• Applying ecclesiological conclusions to these two characteristics of Jesus—Messiah of the poor and poor Messiah—we can say that the church as depository of the messianic mission of Jesus, the church which is an extension of the mystery of the kenosis (self-emptying) of the Word, cannot fail to be, first of all and in a privileged way, in a clear sense, the church of the Poor in two ways: as a church before all of the poor, for the poor, sent for the salvation of the poor, and in another way as a poor Church.

• For this reason, the question of the church of the poor couldn't be just one more subject for the Council to consider, but should be the general and synthetizing subject of the whole Council.[21]

"The Pact of the Catacombs"

Cardinal Lercaro's words bore fruit. As the council drew to a close on November 16, 1965, forty bishops met at night

---

[20] Ibid.
[21] Ibid.

in the Domitilla Catacombs outside Rome. In that holy place of Christian martyrs they celebrated the Eucharist and signed a document that expressed their personal commitment as bishops to the ideals of the council under the suggestive title "The Pact of the Catacombs." Franciscan bishop Boaventura Kloppenburg inserted a transcript in the *Chronicle of Vatican II*. He titled the document "The Pact of the Servant and Poor Church."[22] It is known that the bishops were led by Archbishop Hélder Câmara of Recife, Brazil, one of the most widely respected twentieth-century champions of justice and peace. Cardinal Roger Etchegaray, who later served as honorary president of the Pontifical Council of Justice and Peace, was another signatory.

In this pact the bishops committed themselves to ideals of poverty and simplicity, leaving their palaces and living in individual houses or apartments in increasing closeness with the poor. We have to recognize that although Dom Hélder Câmara and Dom Manuel Larrain did not achieve all that they hoped for in the council, their efforts did make a deep spiritual and prophetic impact.

"The Pact of the Catacombs" is a challenge to their "brothers in the episcopacy" to embrace a life of poverty, in order to build a church that is "poor and servant," as suggested by Pope John XXIII. The signatories included many Brazilian and Latin Americans, along with others who later endorsed it. They all agreed to live in evangelical poverty, to reject all symbols or privileges of power, and to put the poor at the center of their pastoral ministry.

The text, which we reproduce below, shows fully the spirit of a church along the lines that Cardinal Lercaro announced: a church for the poor and a poor church.[23]

---

[22] Available on the http://www.sedosmission.org website.

[23] According to Brazilian historian José Oscar Beozzo, there were thirty-nine bishops present, but there are two lists. For a more precise view, see José Oscar Beozzo "Nota sobre os participantes da celebração do Pacto das Catacumbas," available in Portuguese at http://nucleodememoria.vrac.puc-rio.br;

The Pact of the Catacombs: A Poor Servant Church

We, bishops assembled in the Second Vatican Council, are conscious of the deficiencies of our lifestyle in terms of evangelical poverty. Motivated by one another in an initiative in which each of us has tried avoid ambition and presumption, we unite with all our brothers in the episcopacy and rely above all on the grace and strength of Our Lord Jesus Christ and on the prayer of the faithful and the priests in our respective dioceses. Placing ourselves in thought and in prayer before the Trinity, the Church of Christ, and all the priests and faithful of our dioceses, with humility and awareness of our weakness, but also with all the determination and all the strength that God desires to grant us by his grace, we commit ourselves to the following:

We will try to live according to the ordinary manner of our people in all that concerns housing, food, means of transport, and related matters. See Matthew 5,3; 6,33ff; 8,20.

1.   We renounce forever the appearance and the substance of wealth, especially in clothing (rich vestments, loud colors) and symbols made of precious metals (these signs should certainly be evangelical). See Mark 6,9; Matthew 10,9–10; Acts 3.6 (Neither silver nor gold).

2.   We will not possess in our own names any properties or other goods, nor will we have bank accounts or the like. If it is necessary to possess something, we will place everything in the name of the diocese or of social or charitable works. See Matthew 6,19–21; Luke 12,33–34.

3.   As far as possible we will entrust the financial and material running of our diocese to a commission of competent lay persons who are aware of their apostolic role, so that we can be less administrators and more pastors and apostles. See Matthew 10,8; Acts 6,1–7.

4.   We do not want to be addressed verbally or in writing with names and titles that express prominence and power (such

---

idem, *Pacto das catacumbas para uma Igreja serva e pobre* (São Paulo: Paulinas, 2015). See also Xabier Pikaza, *El Pacto de las catacumbas* (Estella: Verbo Divino, 2015; English version in preparation).

as Eminence, Excellency, Lordship). We prefer to be called by the evangelical name of "Father." See Matthew 20,25–28; 23,6–11; John 13,12–15).

5.   In our communications and social relations we will avoid everything that may appear as a concession of privilege, prominence, or even preference to the wealthy and the powerful (for example, in religious services or by way of banquet invitations offered or accepted). See Luke 13,12–14; 1 Corinthians 9,14–19.

6.   Likewise we will avoid favoring or fostering the vanity of anyone at the moment of seeking or acknowledging aid or for any other reason. We will invite our faithful to consider their donations as a normal way of participating in worship, in the apostolate, and in social action. See Matthew 6,2–4; Luke 15,9–13; 2 Corinthians 12,4.

7.   We will give whatever is needed in terms of our time, our reflection, our heart, our means, etc., to the apostolic and pastoral service of workers and labor groups and to those who are economically weak and disadvantaged, without allowing that to detract from the welfare of other persons or groups of the diocese. We will support lay people, religious, deacons, and priests whom the Lord calls to evangelize the poor and the workers by sharing their lives and their labors. See Luke 4,18–19; Mark 6,4; Matthew 11,4–5; Acts 18,3–4; 20,33–35; 1 Corinthians 4,12; 9,1–27.

8.   Conscious of the requirements of justice and charity and of their mutual relatedness, we will seek to transform our works of welfare into social works based on charity and justice, so that they take all persons into account, as a humble service to the responsible public agencies. See Matthew 25,31–46; Luke 13,12–14; 13,33–34.

9.   We will do everything possible so that those responsible for our governments and our public services establish and enforce the laws, social structures, and institutions that are necessary for justice, equality, and the integral, harmonious development of the whole person and of all persons, and thus for the advent of a new social order, worthy of the children of God. See Acts 2,44–45; 4;32–35; 5,4; 2 Corinthians 8 and 9; 1 Timothy 5,16.

10.   Since the collegiality of the bishops finds its supreme evangelical realization in jointly serving the two-thirds of humanity who

live in physical, cultural, and moral misery, we commit ourselves: a) to support as far as possible the most urgent projects of the episcopacies of the poor nations; and b) to request jointly, at the level of international organisms, the adoption of economic and cultural structures which, instead of producing poor nations in an ever richer world, make it possible for the poor majorities to free themselves from their wretchedness. We will do all this even as we bear witness to the gospel, after the example of Pope Paul VI at the United Nations.

11.   We commit ourselves to sharing our lives in pastoral charity with our brothers and sisters in Christ, priests, religious, and laity, so that our ministry constitutes a true service. Accordingly, we will make an effort to "review our lives" with them; we will seek collaborators in ministry so that we can be animators according to the Spirit rather than dominators according to the world; we will try be make ourselves as humanly present and welcoming as possible; and we will show ourselves to be open to all, no matter what their beliefs. See Mark 8,34–35; Acts 6,1–7; 1 Timothy 3,8–10.

12.   When we return to our dioceses, we will make these resolutions known to our diocesan priests and ask them to assist us with their comprehension, their collaboration, and their prayers. May God help us to be faithful.[24]

This text had a strong influence on liberation theology, which would flourish in the coming years. Besides Dom Hélder Câmara, those who were signatories and committed radically to it included Brazilians Don Antonio Fragoso, from Crateús, Brazil, and Don José Maria Pires, of João Pessoa, affectionately called Don Zumbi because of his strong commitment to the Afro-Brazilian peoples. From His-

---

[24] Jon Sobrino, SJ, "The Urgent Need to Return to Being the Church of the Poor," trans. Fr. Joseph Owens, *National Catholic Reporter*, March 24, 2010, available on the ncronline. org website. The article includes the following: "Editor's Note: This article was written in 2009 for the 100th anniversary of the birth of Bishop Hélder Câmara."

panic America signatories included: Bishop Manuel Larrain, from Talca, Chile; Bishop Marcos Gregorio McGrath, from Panama (Diocese of Santiago de Veraguas); Bishop Leonidas Proaño, from Riobamba, Ecuador; and many others.

The beautiful introductory text and the very concrete commitments listed by the bishops are immediately striking not only because of their radicalism, but also because of the spiritual fire that is present and communicated. These are words full of fervor, clearly demonstrating what Gustavo Gutiérrez, the "father" of liberation theology and the option for the poor, never tires of repeating: the poor are the center of Christian life, and all Christians, including bishops, need a conversion to them.[25] However, the preferential option for the poor, which gives identity and face to this theology, does not begin or depart from a simple critical analysis of reality but rather from a mystical experience, an encounter with the crucified Lord in the face of the poor.

The Poor: The Heart of a Reformed Theology

The option for the poor in the Latin American church was then conceived as having two central meanings:

1. A concrete solidarity with the poor, which moves one to assume their perspective, their interests, their pains, and their desires. This, in turn, implies the commitment of the whole church to embrace "material poverty"[26] and to denounce unjust structures that produce poverty and oppression.

2. A determination to create conditions that allow the poor to emerge as ecclesial subjects, as evangelizing agents

---

[25] Gutiérrez, *A Theology of Liberation*.

[26] CELAM, "Poverty of the Church" (II:5). See also the commentary by P. Trigo, "Ha muerto la Teologia de la Liberación? La realidad actual y sus causas I," *Revista Latinoamericana de Teología* 22 (2005): 45–74.

of the whole church, responsible for the necessary transformations for the establishment of justice and a new society.[27] In fact, as we have stated, liberation theology was never a purely academic theory, but rather an ecclesial practice meant to help the church develop a clearer goal in serving the poor. Liberation theologians were simply trying to return to the source, the core of the gospel that tells us: "blessed are the poor" (Mt 5; Lk 6:20).[28] Christian conversion under that perspective implies and includes, then, not only helping the poor with charitable handouts, but also trying to live like them; to experience—even to a limited extent—what they endure; and to participate and empathize with their suffering and condition. The objective is to help the poor to become artisans of their own history and destiny. As Gutiérrez states:

> When it is lived in authentic imitation of Christ, the witness of poverty does not alienate us from the world at all. . . . Only through concrete acts of love and solidarity can we effectively realize our encounter with the poor and the exploited and through them, with Jesus Christ. To give to them is to say yes to Christ; to refuse them is to reject Christ.[29]

Many questions arose from the Latin American church's attempt to be closer to the poor and to think theologically from that locus. Groups were formed that tried different models of following Christ by following the poor.

---

[27] Carneiro de Andrade, "Opción por los pobres en el magistério."

[28] See the reflections of Gustavo Gutiérrez, *A Theology of Liberation;* and Clodovis Boff and Jorge Pixley, *The Bible, the Church, and the Poor* (Maryknoll, NY: Orbis Books, 1989).

[29] Gustavo Gutiérrez, "Liberation Praxis and Christian Faith," in *Frontiers of Theology in Latin America*, ed. Rosino Gibellini, trans. John Drury (Maryknoll, NY: Orbis Books, 1979), 14.

Nevertheless, other groups, including many middle-class Catholics, rejected the idea of becoming poor as the only way to live their faith and complained that their church was neglecting them. Clodovis Boff, one of the more prominent liberation theologians, came up with a typology that helped broach an understanding of what it means to share the life of the poor, to make a preferential (though not exclusive) option for the poor, while respecting one's state in life, work, and family commitments.

Clodovis Boff stated that every Christian must commit to the option for the poor, because this is the only way truly to follow Jesus Christ.[30] Life circumstances can be, and often are, diverse. However, this mandate for all Christians also has diverse nuances when put into practice.

One can opt for the poor with a *conversion of interests.* A person can hold a respectable position among peers and the public yet still redirect skills, capabilities, and fruits toward the needs of the poor, to help and empower them, thus ensuring a social impact, making structures more just and society more fair.

One can also opt for the poor by *alternating* one's social standing with theirs. That is the case of many Christians, both religious and lay people, who work for a living during the week but on the weekend help in a poor neighborhood. Those who teach at a university can spend holidays living among the poor, teaching classes, building houses, providing free medical consultations or dentistry. To some extent they share in the living conditions of those who are poor, if only for a certain number of hours, days, or weeks.

A third way of living the option for the poor is through *incarnation:* This means to cut ties with one's previous life, including comfort, privacy, time, and money, and go out to share entirely in the life of the poor. There have been many people—lay people, religious, and clergy—who have made

---

[30] Boff and Pixley, *The Bible, the Church, and the Poor.*

this radical option and continue to do so still.[31] As Gustavo Gutiérrez writes with strength and prophetic fire:

> Love of neighbor is an essential component of Christian life. Nevertheless, as long as I apply that term only to the people who cross my path and come asking me for help, my world will remain pretty much the same. Individual almsgiving and social reformism is a type of love that never leaves its own front porch. . . . But the existence of the poor . . . is not neutral on the political level or innocent of ethical implications. Poor people are byproducts of the system under which we live and for which we are responsible. . . . That is why the poverty of the poor is not a summons to alleviate their plight with acts of generosity, but rather a compelling obligation to fashion an entirely different social order.[32]

It is this different social order that many Latin American Christians and theologians mean to build. However, it is not only a sociological, economic, or political effort. In the center of all these efforts, which generated numerous witnesses, prophets, and martyrs, there is God, the God of Jesus Christ and of Christians, who is the cause and the motivation for this whole movement, which arose in Latin America and has spread to other parts of the world.[33]

---

[31] For instance, Dorothy Day, Dorothy Stang, and the three religious and the lay woman murdered in El Salvador (Maura Clarke, Ita Ford, Dorothy Kazel, and Jean Donovan). All the writings of Dorothy Day speak about the radicality with which she lived this option. See, for instance, her autobiography, *The Long Loneliness* (New York: Harper and Row, 1952). See also Jim Forest, *All Is Grace: A Biography of Dorothy Day* (Maryknoll, NY: Orbis Books, 2011).

[32] Gutiérrez, "Liberation Praxis and Christian Faith."

[33] Liberation theology also became widely known and respected in the United States and Europe. Many of its major texts have been translated into many languages, including Italian, French, English, and German.

The Poor: Victims of Dehumanization, Beloved by God

In the context of liberation theology, as we have seen, "the poor" refers to the oppressed, to the victims of a world structure that is unjust and that therefore fails to correspond to the justice desired by God. The option for the poor, then, should not be understood as something different from the option for the victims of racism, or of gender discrimination, or of cultural marginalization. The option for the poor is ultimately an option for justice. The most renowned liberation theologians have emphasized the tremendous interpellation that the existence of poverty, conceived in this sense, represents for humanity, situating this problem at the very center of theological thought. They have endeavored to discover the causes of poverty and the means to fight it. They have promoted the creation of base ecclesial communities, which, through reading of the Bible, help the poor to see their situation more clearly and to make the necessary decisions to transform it. Moreover, they have fought not so much against atheism as against idolatry as the principal enemy of faith. This idolatry deifies consumerism, wealth, power—in sum, everything on which the modern capitalist society is based.[34]

The theology of Leonardo Boff, for example, proposes a radical rupture with the logic of the capitalist system, one that aims to liberate the poor and the oppressed.[35] Jon Sobrino's theology identifies the poor with the victim, proclaiming the necessity of a political holiness that would assume the risks of an incarnation in the life of the poor in order

---

[34] See Jon Sobrino, "The Epiphany of the God of Life in Jesus of Nazareth," in *The Idols of Death and the God of Life,* ed. Pablo Richard et al. (Maryknoll, NY: Orbis Books, 1983), 66–102.

[35] Boff advocates for this thesis in many different books. See, for example, *Jesus Christ Liberator: A Critical Christology for Our Times* (Maryknoll, NY: Orbis Books, 1978); *Trinity and Society* (Maryknoll, NY: Orbis Books, 1988); *Ecclesiogenesis: The Base Communities Reinvent the Church* (Maryknoll, NY: Orbis Books, 1986).

to fight for their liberation.[36] Following closely the life and memory of Oscar Romero, the archbishop of San Salvador who was assassinated while celebrating the Eucharist in 1980, Sobrino argues that "political holiness is historically necessary today for the poor to receive the good news and for history to move toward the coming of God's kingdom." It is necessary as well in order for the church to return to the gospel and to show the world a more credible face, which it can do only by means of a radical and effective love of the poor.[37] So, as we can see, the option for the poor is not only directed toward a personal level (conversion, perfection of Christian life), but also to political and structural goals concerning society and church.

From the beginning liberation theology has understood itself as the bearer of a qualified word that added to others in history, can contribute to the liberation of the poor and oppressed of every kind. However, it has always maintained very clearly that there will be no real liberation unless the poor themselves raise their voices freely and express themselves directly and creatively in society and history.

Liberation theologians believe that the attitude that liberates the poor from their poverty, the afflicted from their affliction, is the one that is creative exactly in and through its humility. Only through renunciation of pride and power can one learn to go beyond merely giving material things in order to satisfy immediate needs. Liberation theology—translated into attitude and action—intends to give to those who suffer injustice the possibility of regaining their human

---

[36] See, for example, Sobrino's most widely known works: *Christology at the Crossroads: A Latin American Approach* (Maryknoll, NY: Orbis Books, 1978); *Christ the Liberator: A View from the Victims* (Maryknoll, NY: Orbis Books, 2001); *Jesus in Latin America* (Maryknoll, NY: Orbis Books, 1987); and *True Church and the Poor* (Maryknoll, NY: Orbis Books, 1984).

[37] Jon Sobrino, *Spirituality of Liberation: Toward Political Holiness* (Maryknoll, NY: Orbis Books, 1988), 86.

dignity, of fully assuming their mission of transforming their history and destiny.

In fact, the careful and loving service to the poor is the source, the core of the gospel of Jesus Christ, who says "blessed are the poor" (Mt 5; Lk 6:20). According to Matthew the only principle of salvation is based not on rituals, moral norms, obedience to commandments, or profession of dogmatic formulas, but on the practice of giving bread to the hungry, water to the thirsty, and clothing to the naked.

The poverty of the other—whom the Bible specifies in such categories as the poor, the widow, the orphan, the foreigner—has to be, in a mandatory way, the main concern of every single disciple of Jesus Christ. As Nicolai Berdyaev, the Russian-émigré Christian thinker observed, "When I am hungry, it is a physical problem. When my neighbor is hungry, it is a spiritual problem."

It is not the goal for Christians to idealize poverty or the poor, but rather to take it on as it is—evil—and to protest against it and to struggle to abolish it. The poor are not sentimentalized or idealized figures; they are those who are marginalized by society, oppressed in every way, exploited and not allowed to live fully because of that oppression. God identifies with those men and women in the person of the incarnate Son, who took our vulnerable flesh and submitted himself to all the negative situations human beings endure. In serving the poor, Christians and non-Christians are serving their Lord, sacramentally present in them: "Truly I tell you, just as you did it to one of the least of these who are members of my family, you did it to me" (Mt 25:40). In spite of loving all creatures equally, making no exception for human beings, God, Father of Jesus, identifies in a very special way with the poor. That means that God is with those who suffer any kind of poverty or injustice, living in them, suffering in them, becoming visible through them. That makes them—men and women who suffer discrimination, oppression, or violence—God's sacrament in history and society. They include not only those economically or materially poor, or those simply "poor in spirit." The biblical concept of "the poor" refers rather to the oppressed, to the victims of a world organization that fails to correspond to the justice desired by God. The option for the poor, then, should not be understood as something different from the option for *all* victims of oppression or exclusion in an unjust world.

In this commitment Christians may work with brothers and sisters belonging to other religious traditions or even with nonbelievers. All of them will be practicing *caritas* when they practice works of justice and mercy. Such works are such an integral part of the kingdom of God that whenever they are performed God's glory is proclaimed and the kingdom grows.

The Poor: A Theocentric and Theological Question

If there is a point on which all the currents and tendencies of liberation theology agree, it is that the option for the poor is theocentric. For liberation theology, in other words, the reason to opt for the poor is simply God, not an ideology, a theory, or a result of social analysis.[38] While affirming categorically and in accordance with biblical revelation the universality of God's revelation and love, liberation theology contends that God is nonetheless revealed with special radicalism in the field of justice. God sides with justice, taking up completely the cause of those who have been wronged. Those who believe in this God, in the God of Revelation, the God of the Bible, the God of Jesus Christ, have no other path to follow than that of the option for the poor.[39] So together with the universality of God, Christian revelation announces also the partiality of the same God.

In the Jewish and Christian scriptures it is clear that there is no experience of God if there is not, at the same

---

[38] See Gustavo Gutiérrez, *The God of Life* (Maryknoll, NY: Orbis Books, 1991).

[39] See Ronaldo Muñoz, *The God of Christians* (Maryknoll, NY: Orbis Books, 1994), chap. 2.

time, justice to human beings, mostly to those who are oppressed or not allowed to live fully and deeply. Injustice and idolatry, then, go together, one with the other. By the same token, faith and justice go hand in hand. When people fail to relate correctly with God, they also fail to relate correctly to one another, and vice versa.

During the days of Moses, God established some guidelines under the Law to help the poor. Exodus 22 and 23 contain instructions to the people of Israel to help the aliens, widows, orphans, and the poor. God protects their property, warns again against showing favoritism, and sets up a system of gleaning to help prevent starvation and malnutrition (Ex 23:10–12). He is the *go'el*—the helper, the spokesperson, the advocate, the one who speaks for those who have no one to speak for them.

In Leviticus 25:8–43 God institutes the Year of Jubilee, to be practiced every fifty years. God says to the people of Israel:

> Do not take advantage of each other, but fear your God. . . . If one of your countrymen becomes poor and is unable to support himself among you, help him as you would an alien or a temporary resident, so he can continue to live among you. Do not take interest of any kind from him, but fear your God, so that your countrymen may continue to live among you. . . . If one of your countrymen becomes poor among you and sells himself to you, do not make him work as a slave. He is to be treated as a hired worker or a temporary resident among you; he is to work for you until the Year of Jubilee. (Lev 25:17, 35–36, 39–40)

In Deuteronomy 15 we see God's intention that the people's debts will be canceled every seven years. This was appropriately called the Year for Canceling Debts.

God's great love for the poor is so much a part of the divine identity that it is reflected in many of God's names:

- Defender of the fatherless and widows (Deut 10:18; Pss 10:16–18; 40:17; 68:5; Jer 22:16)
- Protector of the poor (Ps 12:5)
- Rescuer of the poor (1 Sam 2; Pss 35:10; 72:4; Isa 19:20; Jer 20:13)
- Provider of the poor (Pss 68:10; 146:7; Isa 41:17)
- Savior of the poor (Pss 34:6; 109:31)
- Refuge of the poor (Ps 14:6; Isa 25:4).

For those who bless the poor, God promises blessings in return (Ps 41:1–3; 112; Prov 14:21; 14:31; 19:17; 22:9; 28:27; Isa 58:6–10). God also promises to judge those who oppress the poor (Deut 27:19; Prov; 17:5; 21:13; 22:16; 28:27; Isa 10:1–4; Ez 16:49; 18:12–13).

Jesus is no less radical in his teachings about wealth and poverty, offering severe admonitions against accumulation of goods. "Do not accumulate for yourselves treasures on earth, where moth and rust destroy and where thieves break in and steal. However, accumulate for you treasures in heaven, where moth and rust do not destroy, and thieves do not break in and steal. For where your treasure is, there your heart will be also" (Mt 6:19–21). A free heart is a heart that is not tied to earthly goods, but, on the contrary, is founded on love for God and compassion and solidarity with others.

In addition, Jesus' recommendations to his disciples presuppose a way of life based on simplicity and detachment from material things. The graciousness of creation reflects the graciousness of God, who gives the grace of life and invites all creatures to seek life in abundance.

Therefore I tell you, do not worry about your life, what you will eat or drink, or about your body, what you will wear. Isn't there more to life than food and more to the body than clothing? Look at the birds in the sky: They do not sow, or reap, or gather into barns, yet your heavenly Father feeds them. Aren't you more valuable than they are? And which of you by worrying can add even one hour to his life? Why do you worry about clothing? Think about how the flowers of the field grow; they do not work or spin. Yet I tell you that not even Solomon in all his glory was clothed like one of these! And if this is how God clothes the wild grass, which is here today and tomorrow is tossed into the fire to heat the oven, won't he clothe you even more, you people of little faith? So then, do not worry saying, "What will we eat?" "What will we drink?" or "What will we wear?" For the unconverted pursue these things, and your heavenly Father knows that you need them. Above all, pursue his kingdom and righteousness, and all these things will be given to you as well. So then, do not worry about tomorrow, for tomorrow will worry about itself. Today has enough trouble of its own. (Mt 6:25–34)

Here is the root of the gospel assertion: "blessed are the poor!" (Mt 5:1) They are blessed because they know not only their dependence on God, but also their interdependence on one another. The poor are ready and well equipped for total confidence in God and at the same time the most radical solidarity with others. The poor rest their security not on things but on people. They know they can survive only if they trust and collaborate with one another, helping each other at any time and in any situation. They do not place their trust in competition but in cooperation. Finally, the poor listen to the gospel as good news and not as threatening and judging news. They can respond to the call of God with fullness of heart, for they have very little to lose and are ready for anything.

Because they are at the very core of the gospel message, the poor have been at the center of Christian social teaching from the time of early church fathers up to the present. In the middle of the twentieth century Pope John XXIII at the

Second Vatican Council defined the church as the church of the poor. Now, Pope Francis puts this theme at the core of his pontificate. This is the track that Latin American theology has walked and followed for all five decades following Vatican II.

What was most important about liberation theology was not the work of highly educated priests and scholars, but the social organization, or reorganization, of church practice through the model of Christian base ecclesial communities. Those small communities—gathered usually outside churches and parishes and formed by people of the grassroots, where the Bible could be discussed and celebration could happen—were the model of how together the poor can find a path for their liberation. The communities were especially active in rural parts of Latin America, where parish priests were not always available. By the 1980s it was estimated that there were eighty thousand base ecclesial communities operating in Brazil alone. Today, this number has radically diminished, but in the poorest and more isolated parts of the continent these communities are still very active.

Considered a "new way of being church," an alternative to the traditional parish, these communities were and are formed by poor people and by pastoral agents who identify with them and want to share their life. This shows that liberation theology, despite the doctrinal codification by Gutiérrez, Boff, and others, has tried in practice to be a bottom-up movement, with biblical interpretation and liturgical practice designed by lay practitioners themselves. The biblical circles, embryos of the base ecclesial communities, confronted facts with the word of God to extract from them a way of transforming unjust reality.

Furthermore, with its emphasis on the preferential option for the poor, practice was and is as important as belief, if not more so; the movement was said to emphasize ortho-praxis over orthodoxy. Again, this is nothing new, something that liberation theology created. Rather, it is the practical translation of the biblical principle that faith operates by charity, or, as the epistle of James states: "What good is it . . . if you say you have faith but do not have works? . . . For just as the body without the spirit is dead, so faith without works is also dead" (Jas 2:14, 26). To listen to the word of God can only bring one to practice the will of God. That was what the base ecclesial communities, and the liberation theologians who accompanied them, tried to do.

Conclusion

All this movement of the church toward those at the margins began to generate changes in ecclesial style itself. It is impossible to opt for the poor from a distance. God models the path to the poor, the method, the way to serve them and to be with them in self-emptying kenosis, by becoming human flesh. In a similar fashion the option for the poor is an incarnated spirituality that requires an exodus from one's own habits, comforts, possessions, and time.

Liberation theology, by putting service to the poor at the center of the church's life and action, did not make a purely sociological or political choice. This was a theological choice, backed by the entire history of the church. Liberation theologians affirm that it is necessary to opt preferentially for the poor because God did so. God revealed himself as the God of the poor, who is drawn close by the cries of people in distress; who speaks for the poor, widows, orphans, and foreigners; who abandons divine privileges to assume our vulnerable and mortal flesh, obedient unto death on the cross. The option for the poor is not motivated by the desire to create a political party or political structures—even if those mediations could seem useful and reasonable—but to do God's will and to advance God's reign. The fruits of that option will be seen in structural changes and the transformation of reality to reflect better God's heart. And it will be seen as the poor assume the power to take their liberation into their own hands. On that day liberation theologians will be able to exclaim in praise and gratitude, as Jesus of Nazareth did in his time:

"I thank you, Father, Lord of heaven and earth, because you have hidden these things from the wise and the intelligent and have revealed them to infants." (Mt 11:25)

3.

Gender and Human Rights in Latin America

The winds of change for women's emancipation in the Christian West, and in Latin America in particular, did not blow initially from inside the churches. They came from within the lay process of secularization through concrete and mundane struggles (for the right to vote, wages, working hours, sexuality, and rights of the body). Through these struggles women began to extricate themselves from the domestic private space where they had been confined and move into the public space, as political and economic actors engaged in changing social structures and in economic and cultural production.

The voice of women, heard in Latin American Christian communities, does not date back more than five decades. After the great event of the Second Vatican Council, the

This chapter originally appeared as "Theology, Women, and Rights of the Poor (A Reading of the Latin-American Itinerary)," in *Feminist Catholic Theological Ethics: Conversations in the World Church,* ed. Linda Hogan and A. E. Orobator (Maryknoll, NY: Orbis Books, 2014). Minor editing changes have been made for this volume.

female voice began to be heard more and more, effectively occupying spaces inside the church. Women coordinated communities at different levels, questioned the denial of women's access to priestly ministry, and produced theoretical reflections about religious experience and the doctrinal contents of Christian faith. The fact is, today it is not possible to do theology in our continent without taking into account women's contribution.

This chapter covers the main steps of this itinerary by demonstrating that each step of theological growth was, at the same time, both a feminist struggle and a struggle for wider human rights. First, we see how theology built by women in Latin America was, in its initial phase, very close to liberation theology, connected to the question of the poor and to their struggle to assume their rightful place as agents of history. Second, I show how, in a second phase, women theologians started in our continent to do the work of re-reading Christian theology more widely, not just from their experience as women, but vindicating, through their right to be different, the authority to pronounce a different theological word. Third, I show how advances in feminist theology and in gender reflection altered the direction of Latin American theology. Fourth, I also show how the question of feminism and the rights of women in feminist theology are intertwined with the question of land and ecology, thus generating the important theological stream named eco-feminism. Finally, I reflect on the empowerment of women, which entails many delicate but inescapable themes, such as embodied life, reproductive rights, and the question of ordained ministries.

The Poor as the Cradle of Theological Work for Feminist and Liberation Theologies

Theology produced by women in Latin America originated around 1968, when the Latin American bishops conference gathered at Medellín to evaluate the reception of Vatican II within the continent. The key to this conference was the inseparability between the announcement of the gospel and the struggle for justice. Medellín's three steps were the connection between evangelization and the struggle against oppression and injustice; the connection between theology and critical analysis of socioeconomic and political reality; and the formation and strengthening of base ecclesial communities inspired by their reading of the Bible in order to transform unjust social conditions. These steps opened new ways for theological reflection to find, in the poor and marginalized of the continent a new subject as starting point.

Building on this, during the 1970s Latin American women began to explore theology within the Latin American churches from the point of view of their strong interdependence with the poor and the preferential option for the poor. They drew inspiration from their sisters in the North, who were opening up discussions about the possibility of thinking and speaking "beyond God the Father" and the patriarchalism that was dominant in theology.[1] Latin American women theologians saw, as a strong and beautiful challenge, the possibility of inaugurating a theology in which they could participate as producers, not only as consumers. Nevertheless, Latin American theology done by women was not identical to feminist theology done in the Northern Hemisphere. It was inseparable from the preferential option for the poor.[2]

The women who, in those years, began taking theology courses and undertaking the adventure of creating their own reflection about God's mystery and revelation, were not

---

[1] See Mary Daly, *Beyond God the Father: Toward a Philosophy for Woman's Liberation* (Boston: Beacon Press, 1973).

[2] Silvana Suaiden, "Questões contemporâneas para a teologia—Provocações sob a ótica de gênero," in SOTER [Brazilian Society for Theology and Religious Studies], *Genero e Teologia. Interpelações e perspectivas* (São Paulo: Loyola, 2003), 147.

moved only by their personal desires. Those early pioneers were driven to dare the impossible, to venture into a world that had been dominated by men and, almost entirely, by celibate clergy. This was a world where feminine thinking and presence only had an indirect entry. This was the world where the "crazy" ones of that first moment began to articulate their reflections and dared to take their first theological steps.[3]

However, there was also the challenge of reality. Women who intended to do theology in this initial moment had their eyes turned to the reality of the poor, and they perceived that theology should be done in a close dialogue with the social sciences. They also recognized a reality that was later called the feminization of poverty.[4] A poor person, who is also a woman, is doubly poor, since her female condition adds to her marginalized condition, making her life even more complex and difficult. Thus, a new solidarity emerged in Latin America, one that linked women theologians with poor women who were in grassroots communities.

Starting with desires and dreams, the status of women theologians began to take on a concrete reality. Besides their presence in grassroots ministry, women gradually developed space for their work in universities and institutes of theology, obtaining the academic degrees that enabled them to have an equal voice with their male colleagues. This represented a whole journey, a search for recognition, presence, and visibility in spaces that had been predominantly masculine. It was an attempt to attain citizenship

---

[3] *Crazy* in English translates the Spanish *locas*. I allude here to the Mothers of the Plaza de Mayo in Argentina, who were routinely dismissed by the dictatorship as "las locas."

[4] The introduction of this concept is given by the North American thinker Diane Pearce in an article published in 1978. For her, the feminization of poverty is a process that develops when women, without the support of a husband or partner, must assume responsibility for the care and well being of their children.

and legitimacy through a different and alternative way of doing theology—a way in which hearts, minds, and bodies were united in a fertile and harmonic dance, resulting in a fresh reflection about faith.

During the 1990s, Latin American female theologians felt the impact of the fall of utopias and the crisis of liberation theology, their cradle. Socioeconomic and political questions dominated their agendas. Like all intellectuals in that historical moment, they had to confront reality and try to search for new directions in their method of doing theology. They did so. Faithful to the originating intuition—that faith and justice go together and are inseparable—female theologians were sufficiently perceptive to realize that times were changing. The context of that moment showed it was necessary to pay attention to other fields of learning and science, such as anthropology, philosophy, and natural sciences, in order to find appropriate partners for their reflection about revelation and faith.

Rethinking Theological Concepts from Women's Perspective

The result of this process was the desire to rethink the full range of major theological themes from the perspective of women. Ivone Gebara, in what she has identified as a second stage in the trajectory of Latin American feminist theology, calls this the "feminization of theological concepts."[5] Although there was an increased presence of women in the spaces of academic reflection, theological concepts remained patriarchal. Women sought a theology with a feminine face, soul, and configuration, that is, a female perspective of theology able to stress the importance of rediscovering God's feminine dimensions. Here began a more fruitful and solid

---

[5] Ivone Gebara, "III Semana Teológica—Construyendo nuestras Teologias Feministasm," *Tópicos 90—Cuadernos de Estudios* (Chile: Ediciones Ruhue, September 1993), 71–124.

stage of publications, with women theologians trying to revisit and to rethink the great treatises of dogmatic theology and the Bible itself, always from a point of departure in women's experience and feelings.[6]

Latin American women theologians acknowledged their debt to the work of their North American sisters. However, they also identified an important distinction. They were not motivated primarily by the fight for equality and against sexism. Instead, they struggled to build an inclusive discourse rooted in the distinctive experience and perspective of women. In this stage of the process there was a tendency to avoid the words *feminism* and *feminist.* Preference was given to expressions like *theology from the perspective of women* or *theology made by women* or *theology from women.*[7]

Many doctoral dissertations and academic papers were produced along these lines. In the area of systematic theology many works reflected on Jesus' relationship with women; on the maternal face of God; or even on an inclusive and participatory model of church, in which women would be seen as agents, producers of symbolic goods, and not only as passive consumers.[8]

---

[6] Relevant publications are too numerous to cite; for an extensive bibliography, see Maria Pilar Aquino, *Our Cry for Life: Feminist Theology from Latin America* (Maryknoll, NY: Orbis Books, 1993). Note also the extraordinary work of Elsa Tamez, who has not only thought about the Bible in a new way but has organized several publications to make known the work of her fellow Latin American theologians; see Elsa Tamez, ed., *Through Her Eyes: Women's Theology from Latin America* (Maryknoll, NY: Orbis Books, 1989).

[7] See Tamez, *Through Her Eyes.*

[8] A. M. Tependino, *As discípulas de Jesus* (Petrópolis: Vozes, 1990); M. C. Bingemer, "A perspectiva da Trindade na ótica da mulher," *Revista Eclesiástica Brasileira [REB]* 46 (1986): 73–99; D. Brunelli, *Libertação da Mulher: Um Desafio para a Vida Religiosa na Igreja Latino Americana* (Rio de Janeiro: Publicações CRB, 1988).

This way of doing theology continues. It is not isolated from the theological work of women worldwide. It finds conceptual affinities with some European theologians of the same generation and moves among the key concepts of reciprocity, non-duality, and relationality, always pursuing dialogue with male theologians and the theological community as a whole.[9] The claims of this kind of theology no longer aligned with early feminism, whose main struggle was for equality. Latin American women sought another right: the right to be different. Even in dialogue with the work of women in other areas of knowledge,[10] women theologians emphasize the identity of the woman as "other," different from men. Women who claim this identity, even in the way they feel and think about God, produce a theology that differs from a feminist theology built on the paradigm of equality.

Another stream of Latin American theologians wished to take a step beyond the discourse of difference and reciprocity. They felt the need for a more fundamental critique and a radical change in the concept of God and its relation with women's identity. These theologians took the position that the emphasis on women's difference reinforced stereotypes of women as maternal, sensitive, weak, and frail.

Inside that movement, in discussions around the issue of female identity, there were two possible directions: the first insisted on the affirmation of difference, and the second sought to resist the idealization or essentialization of those differences, understanding them as arising within a particular culture and history in which they continue to operate, and in which they are maintained. Debates over

---

[9] I identify among European theologians influential names such as Giulia Paola di Nicola, Georgette Blaquierre, Kari Elisabeth Borresen.

[10] I think, for instance, of R. Darcy De Oliviera, *Elogio da diferença o feminino emergente* (São Paulo: Brasiliense, 1991).

these issues contributed to the next stage in Latin American women's theology.

Taking Gender Perspective Seriously

Latin American feminist theology in the second half of the 1990s faced major challenges that forced it to review some of its presuppositions. One of these came from the need to bridge the gap with feminist theology elsewhere in the world, as well as with Latin American feminist reflection as it was developing in other areas of knowledge.[11]

At this stage theologians were challenged to rethink issues of female identity, anthropology, cosmology, and theology, which had been historically dominated by patriarchal discourse. Feminist theology arose as a radical change to the way we reflect on the data of revelation and the texts of scripture, but also to the way we think about the world and relationships among people, nature, and divinity.

It became clear to the new generations of theologians that it was not possible to build a theology recycled out of old patches without triggering the birth of something truly new. In feminist theology (now that we are no longer afraid to take that name), the intention is to bring forward fundamental questions that challenge the very structure of theological thought as it has developed up till the present. This was not a theology from the point of view or the perspective of women, presented as an addendum or as a separate subdivision of official theology, as defined by male theologians, but a substantive challenge to all dominant theology.[12] Thus, Latin American women theologians have introduced new methods of addressing the Bible, revelation, and dogma.

---

[11] See Maria Carmelita de Freitas, *Genero e teologia: Interpelações e perspectivas* (São Paulo: Loyola, 2003), 23.

[12] See Silvia Regina de Lima Silva, "Teologia feminista LatinoAmericana," in Portuguese at http://ejesus.com.br. See also Ivone Gebara, "Entre os limites da filosofia e da teologia feminista," in SOTER, *Genero e teologia,* 153–70.

As liberation theology widened the range of interest to include other issues that were not strictly socioeconomic and political, but included issues of ecology, culture, the crisis of modernity, gender, race, and ethnicity, so Latin American feminist theology found, through the gender perspective, a most appropriate angle from which to build its reflection and discourse. The commitment to include those on the margins of society was not lost. But the problem was, perhaps more than ever, to challenge mainstream theology. "The poor" as object of reflection and investigation, who had been the quintessential theological subject in Latin American theology in the 1970s and 1980s, were now identified as those excluded from the benefits of social progress and welfare. These excluded ones now have more diversified faces than before and form a much larger and complex picture that challenges theology in multiple directions. Ivone Gebara, a major voice of this new phase, says: "Liberation theology, offering a collective vision of God and emphasizing the social nature of sin did not change the patriarchal anthropology and cosmology on which Christianity is based."[13]

What became necessary was a qualitative leap in order to achieve the liberation of half of humanity. Gebara defined that leap in feminist theology:

> To speak of God and of gender issues is to make a double claim: first, it is to say that what we say about God is connected to our historical experience, our life experience. Then, our same idea of God, and our relationship with him/her or his/her mystery, is marked by what we call . . . the social and cultural construction of gender.[14]

---

[13] Ivone Gebara, "Teologia Cósmica: Ecofeminismo e Panenteísmo," in *Folha Mulher, Projeto Sofia: Mulher, Teologia e Cidadania* (Rio de Janeiro: ISER, n. 8, Ano IV, 1994): 70–75.

[14] Ivone Gebara, *Rompendo o silencio: Uma fenomenologia feminista do mal* (Petrópolis: Vozes, 2000), 218.

That is how other feminist struggles—those present in first-world theologies, in Latin America, and in social and human sciences—became interesting to theologians.[15] Topics such as embodiment; sexuality; and morality, including all those hot and sensitive issues in reproductive rights and all that pertains to Christian morality (the mystery of the human body, its functions, its vocation, and its mystery created by God). All of this became part of the agenda of Latin American feminist theology. In that field, we must recognize that Protestant theologians, whose church structures are very different, took larger steps than their Catholic sisters.[16] That is also how ecofeminist theology emerged and developed at a continental level.[17] Currently, in Latin America, only a few theologians have written extensively about ecofeminism.[18] However, openness and attention to this new interdisciplinary field of reflection has enabled Latin American

[15] See, for example, Maria Pilar Aquino and Maria José Rosado-Nunes, eds., *Feminist Intercultural Theology: Latina Explorations for a Just World* (Maryknoll, NY: Orbis Books, 2007).

[16] W. Deifelt, "Derechos reproductivos en América Latina. Un análisis crítico y teológico a partir de la realidad del Brasil," in *Población y Salud Reproductiva*, ed. Manuel Quintero (Quito: Ediciones CLAI, 1999), 31–49; "Temas e metodologias da teologia feminista," in *Gênero e teologia*, 171–86; Marga Ströher, Wanda Deifelt, and André Musskopf, eds., *À flor da pele: Ensaios sobre gênero e corporeidade* (São Leopoldo Sinodal/CEBI, 2004). See also the more ecumenical work of Paulo Fernando Carneiro de Andrade, ed., *Corporeidade e Teologia* (SOTER/Paulinas, 2007) and many issues of *Revista de Estudos Feministas* from Universidad de Santa Catarina, Brasil.

[17] *Ecofeminism* reflects the synthesis of environmentalism (or ecology) and feminism. It is the theory that seeks the end to all forms of oppression. It relates and connects the domination of race, gender, social class, and domination of nature, of the "other" (the women, children, the elderly, the indigenous). This will be discussed more fully in the next chapter.

[18] See Ivone Gebara, *Longing for Running Water: Ecofeminism and Liberation* (Minneapolis: Fortress Press, 1999). See also Mary Judith Ress, *Ecofeminism in Latin America* (Maryknoll, NY: Orbis Books, 2006).

feminist theology to dialogue with all areas of environmental studies: philosophy, social sciences, environmental law, and so on. The whole area of ecology promises tremendous growth for the future. Any reflection on ecology in relation to land rights and nature is spliced with reflection on women's rights. Since ecofeminism means the end of all forms of domination, theology cannot avoid the concomitant debates; neither can feminist theology, which is becoming the key to liberating women from all forms of oppression.[19]

Women and the Rights of the Body[20]

The theological reflections on woman's sexualized body and gender questions are always important themes in the theological work in Latin America. In a universe where the body is so visible and mainly male, women enter as a troubling factor. It is this—their body being "other" than the body of man—that expresses and marks the experience of God, the thinking and talking about God, in another and distinctive way. The feminine body becomes an important entry point for women's reflection on spirituality, mysticism, and theology—despite the fact that this body has been, on many occasions, a source of discrimination and suffering.

Discrimination against women within the church concerns deeper matters than simple physical power, intellectual formation, and the ability to work. The church is still molded by a strong patriarchal identity. This patriarchal identity underlies the belief in male superiority, reflected

---

[19] See Rosemary Radford Ruether, ed., *Women Healing Earth: Third World Women on Ecology, Feminism, and Religion* (Maryknoll, NY: Orbis Books, 1990), 135–42; idem, *Gaia and God: A Feminist Theology of Earth Healing* (San Francisco: HarperSanFrancisco: 1994). These works have had considerable influence on Latin American feminist theologians.

[20] A substantial part of this section was presented at the World Catholicism Week of the Center for World Catholicism and Intercultural Theology, at De Paul University, Chicago, in April 2010.

not only in an intellectual bias, but also by what we might call an ontological bias. Feminist theology tries to overcome this discrimination through its discourse.

This discrimination is associated strongly—in the field of theology—with the fact that the woman is considered responsible for the entrance of sin into the world, and consequently, the cause of death. Although Pope John Paul II, in his encyclical, *Mulieris dignitatem*, officially denounced this theology, its effects continue. This also explains why mystical experiences of women are regarded with mistrust and suspicion. Many rich mystical experiences of women, touched by God's grace with very intimate messages, remain ignored or in the hands of a few. Examples such as Teresa of Avila are exceptions that confirm the rule.

In the history of the church women were kept at a prudent distance from the sacred and everything surrounding it, such as liturgy and ritual objects, and away from direct mediation with God. While all this required a "pure" body, there was strong doubt that women could aspire to such purity. Despite all progress made, including participation of women in several levels of ecclesial life, there remains a stigma attached to woman as a seductive source of fear, sin, and a threat to male chastity and clergy celibacy.

This terrible fact demands very serious reflection within the church. If it is possible to fight against intellectual discrimination and professional injustice, what can we do with our female bodies? Should women be obliged to deny and ignore our own bodies, our own special bodies created by God, in order to enter into profound communication with the Creator and occupy our proper space in the church? These are questions that demand theological attention.

As it turns toward these concerns, theology enters into dialogue with the wider field of gender studies. Feminist thought, for a long time, has been posing questions connected with woman's body, not only in the area of violence against women, but also in relation to questions regarding reproductive rights and autonomy of the body.[21] In fact, it is a very difficult and delicate field, but a most important one. Feminist theology has been increasingly challenged to act decisively, especially in the field of moral theology, with contributions from women moral theologians opening a new way.[22] Nevertheless, it must be said that this field still has far to go, advancing with creative fidelity and, above all, boldness.

Feminist Theology, Power, and Service: Time for Empowerment?

Although the word *empowerment* only recently entered the vocabulary of Latin American feminist theology, it is becoming increasingly important.[23] The empowerment of women is a fact in society.[24] Feminist theology in all latitudes,

---

[21] See Mary John Mananzan et al., eds., *Women Resisting Violence: A Spirituality of Life* (Maryknoll, NY: Orbis Books, 1996); and Hogan and Orobator, *Feminist Catholic Theological Ethics.*

[22] See Maria Ines Millen, "Os acordes de uma sinfonia. A Moral do Diálogo na Teologia de Bernhard Häring (Juiz de Fora, Brazil: Editar, 2005); idem, "O corpo na perspectiva do gênero," *Horizonte Teológico* 3/5 (2004): 35–56; Maria Joaquina Fernandes Pinto, "Alteridade e bioética: Um novo olhar sobre o outro e sobre a vida," *Repensa* [Rio de Janeiro] 01/01 (2005): 49–65; idem, "Jesus Cristo e a vivência da afetividade: Implicações para vivermos a nossa," in *A Pessoa e a Mensagem de Jesus*, ed. Mário de França Miranda, 76–83 (São Paulo: Loyola, 2002); Norma Falcon, *Recuperación de lo femenino* (Buenos Aires, San Benito, 2008).

[23] *Empowerment* means an approach to work that looks at the delegation of decision-making power, autonomy, and participation. It involves the sharing of power, decentralization, and the challenge to entrenched concentrations of power.

[24] See Maria Conceição Correia Pinto, "Empowerment: Uma prática de serviço social," in *Política Social* (Lisbom: ISCSP, 1998), 247–64.

including in Latin America, is incorporating this principle in its thinking and discourse.[25] Talking theologically about power and empowerment implies, of necessity, the question of women and church ministries.

The question regarding ministries is crucial for Christians today, especially for women, who are always and necessarily lay persons, with no access to ordained ministries. The fact that the Roman Catholic Church does not ordain women—and does not entertain the possibility of doing so, even officially barring debate on the subject—feels like a slap in the face to women who embrace a passion for building the kingdom of God and have a radical dedication to ecclesial service. This impediment, on the one hand, and the enormous needs to which these women are dedicated, on the other, are passionately felt, and they are a source of keen suffering. At the same time the Spirit inspires these women to undertake urgent reflection and action.[26]

The new ecclesial paradigm, which substitutes a church centered on the dualism of clergy-laity with a constantly renewed community and with new dimensions for charisms and ministries born of the Spirit, will allow contemporary

---

[25] See, for instance, the thesis of Luisa Etsuko Tomita, *Corpo e cotidiano: A experiência das mulheres de movimentos populares desafia a teologia feminista da libertação na América Latina* (São Paulo: PUCSP, 2004).

[26] The apostolic letter *Ordinatio Sacerdotalis* (May 1994) reaffirms, through the words of Pope John Paul II, that the church has no authority to ordain women to the priesthood. It further states that this doctrine is based on the continuous tradition of the church. On November 18, 1995, the Congregation for the Doctrine of the Faith published a response to the question raised in many quarters about whether this issue belonged to the deposit of faith. The response of the commission does not attach an ex cathedra status to the pope's statement but says it is doctrine "founded on the written Word of God" and was "from the beginning constantly preserved and put into practice in the tradition of the church," besides being "presented infallibly by the ordinary and universal Magisterium."

women to find a space to realize effective and greater service to the people of God.

In the 1980s, when the fruits of Vatican II began to mature and the church in Latin America had assimilated the conferences of Medellín and Puebla, women dared to challenge an ecclesial situation marked by constant injustice and oppression. Many of them started to take over ministries in their communities. Women assumed responsibility for the coordination of their communities and liturgical celebrations, and they rendered countless services, living out a model of the church in which power is freely shared and decisions are taken more collectively.

The occupation of such an open space began to outline a new paradigm for the church, one that was highly positive and welcomed by the people. In the 1990s, these routes were deepened. The services women rendered testify to the leap, under the inspiration of the Spirit, that has taken place in their ecclesial consciousness.

The Latin American bishops at their 2007 assembly in Aparecida, Brazil, recognized explicitly the contribution of women. The document of Aparecida mentions the importance of women in different ecclesial services, stating for the first time that women should have access to higher levels of decision making in the church.[27]

There is a rich vein for reflection on the future direction of women's ministries. In the awakening of reflection about empowerment, feminist theology may find new ways to enable women to live powerfully in service to God and God's people. For this, it may help to follow another track that has begun to be evident in feminist theology in Latin America: the retrieval of women's historical testimonies and research on their lives, experiences, and thoughts. Increasingly, both male and female theologians are choosing to engage in reflection on the writings and biographies of the great mystics

---

[27] English: CELAM, *The Aparecida Document* (August 5, 2013), no. 458.

of yesterday and today. Their lives and writings scatter seeds of the Spirit in history, always posing a subversive challenge to the establishment. Reflection on these personal stories speaks of a profound and radical experience of the divine that is certainly one way to empower women. Rather than a theology of texts, a theology of testimonies can become a rich challenge for Latin American feminist theology in its attempt to rescue and empower women, who have been marginalized and muted by every social institution.[28]

Conclusion

Feminist theology in Latin America finds itself, today, in a rich and promising moment, nourished by many projects that help and stimulate its growth.[29] In addition to these projects there is a proliferation of graduate programs, with many female students, following feminist lines of investigation. This shows that this theological stream is alive and is a powerful sign in the world and the church.

One thing, at any rate, is clear. Theological reflection of Latin American women has a long road ahead. Even as it is called to communion with sisters from other latitudes, and learning from reciprocal and fertile friendships, it will always bear the mark of its origins.

Consistent with its origins, Latin American feminist theology will remain, as before, the reflection of women on their faith in relation to their identity and being as women: their condition, their bodies, their configuration, their feelings,

---

[28] See Jon Sobrino, *Witnesses to the Kingdom: The Martyrs of El Salvador and the Crucified Peoples* (Maryknoll, NY: Orbis Books, 2003). Sobrino has written extensively on the need for a "theology of witnesses rather than a theology of texts."

[29] For instance, see the project of *Teologanda in Argentina*, available on the http://www.teologanda.com.ar website; or the position of chair for feminist theology at the Universidad Iberoamericana, in Mexico City.

their thinking, and their speech. However, as all of that happens in a context marked by conflict and injustice, it is also a reflection on ecclesial belonging that remains inseparable from citizenship—a tireless effort to connect faith with theology, understanding theology as a human word illuminated by the word of God. This is the way that feminist theology tries to contribute to a more humane world, where human rights are ever more respected and practiced.

4.

The Poor and the Earth

*The world was made
to be a garden and
the vocation of human
being is to be a
gardener.*
—RUBEM ALVES

As we have noted, liberation theology spread widely during the 1970s and 1980s. After 1989, in light of the great changes in the world, liberation theology experienced a major crisis. The fall of the Berlin Wall and the collapse of "real socialism"[1] affected many lay Christians, who were inspired by their faith to commit themselves to the social and political struggle. In Brazil, coincidentally, it was in this same year that the progressive candidate Luis Inácio Lula da Silva lost his first bid for the presidency. Many militants were deeply affected by these facts and entered

---

[1] I use "real socialism" as a literal translation of the Portuguese *socialismo real*. It means not utopic, but concretely tried as political regime in such countries as the Soviet Bloc, Cuba, and so on.

a cycle of depression.[2] This was also the time when the Vatican was voicing great concern about liberation theology; many theologians came under suspicion, and some were subjected to critical notifications or even silencing.[3]

To many, it appeared that the socialist utopia had received the negative judgment of history, leaving only one possible model for society—the capitalist one. Without the alternative represented by the socialist world (the Second World), it was difficult to imagine a way for the so-called Third World to exist apart from the logic of the market economy and a consumerist society.

Now, with historical distance, I think we can evaluate this crisis in a positive sense. It forced liberation theologians to expand their hopes and their perspectives, and to see that the liberation process not only had to do with poverty at a socio-economic-political level, but also at an anthropological and cultural level—with respect to gender, race, and ethnicity. Moreover, liberation came to be understood as not only for human beings but for the whole of creation. Ecological concerns and struggles came to be seen as inseparable from economic and anthropological themes. Ecology, sustainability, and concern for the life of the planet were thus included

---

[2] See Paulo Fernando Carneiro de Andrade, "Encantos e desencantos: a militância do cristão em tempos de crise," in *Fome e Sede de Justiça*, ed. L. C. Suzin, 125–33 (Belo Horizonte, Brazil: Lutador, 2001); idem, "A crise da modernidade e as possibilidades de uma nova militância cristã," in *Terra Prometida. Movimento Social, engajamento cristão e telogia*, ed. L. C. Suzin, 213–24 (Petrópolis: Vozes, 2001).

[3] Among others, Leonardo Boff was silenced and prohibited from publishing, and Gustavo Gutiérrez was in frequent difficulties with the Peruvian hierarchy (Alfred T. Hennelly, *Liberation Theology: A Documentary History* [Maryknoll, NY: Orbis Books, 1990]). Later, Jon Sobrino was the subject of disciplinary notification from the Congregation for the Doctrine of the Faith (Stephen Pope, ed., *Hope and Solidarity: Jon Sobrino's Challenge to Christian Theology* [Maryknoll, NY: Orbis Books, 2008]).

in the liberation theology agenda. Building a habitable world became a challenge that coincided with empowering people to become subjects of their own history.

This movement began with the conviction that to build justice implied building a sustainable world. In addition, there was a realization that everything that does harm to human beings is harmful to the planet as well. Moreover, it was recognized that if the human race continued to destroy nature and life in all its manifestations, soon human beings themselves would cease to exist. The inseparability between the struggle for justice and the struggle for nature and biodiversity became a central component of theological concerns.

The ecological cause is natural to the spirit of liberation. Liberation theology understands human beings to be in communion with the whole cosmos. The same God of life who privileges the poor also reveals the sacred status of creation, which is otherwise emptied and violated by a consumerist society. Liberation theology pleaded then for a new cosmic and solidarity covenant, thus rejecting all domination and exploitation. It gave birth to a true panentheistic spirituality—God present in all things.[4]

Traditional Christian theology, even in its more open and current models, such as liberation theology, was accused of fostering an overly anthropocentric conception of the world and human life in it. The traditional interpretation of the Genesis mandate to "grow and dominate the earth" was considered responsible for this anthropocentric understanding, and thus for humankind's greedy attitude toward nature and creation. Theology was tasked with reversing this picture. In addition, the Christian conscience became increasingly sensitive to the connection between respect and

---

[4] See Leonardo Boff, *Ecology and Liberation: A New Paradigm* (Maryknoll, NY: Orbis Books, 1995). See also the excellent article of João Batista Libanio, "Teologia e Revisão crítica," in *Horizonte* [Belo Horizonte] 11/32 (2013): 1328–56.

reverence for the earth and the cause of liberation proposed in the Bible and the gospel of Jesus.[5]

Throughout the 1990s there was a growing awareness of rising threats to the planet. These threats were not simply theoretical; they had urgent, practical implications. This situation gave rise to new awareness of the dangers facing the earth and all humankind. This prompted concern for reforms leading to lifestyle that were simpler and healthier: in short, a need for sustainable living. The concept of *sustainable living* refers to an individual or societal lifestyle that can be sustained with limited reduction of natural resources. Its adherents most often hold true sustainability as a goal or guide and make lifestyle compromises with respect to things such as methods of transportation, housing, energy sources, and diets, in ways that favor sustainability.[6]

Along with individual measures, there is recognition of the need for structural changes. Modern society, after all, is founded on an ideology of unlimited growth. Ecological consciousness, however, calls for a change of paradigm.[7] Emphasis on growth, along with an increasingly fast-paced life is replaced with slowing down and downsizing. This approach has economic implications, to be sure, but also ethical and political dimensions. It was formed during the 1970s, partially based on Nicholas Georgescu-Roegen's *The Entropy Law and the Economic Process.*[8]

This posits the idea that economic growth—understood as a constant growing of the gross national product (GNP)—is ultimately unsustainable for the global ecosystem. This idea is opposed to the dominant economic paradigm that

---

[5] See Lynn White Jr., "The Historical Roots of Our Ecological Crisis," *Science* 155 (1967): 1203–7; Sally McFague, *The Body of God* (Minneapolis, MN: Fortress Press, 1993).

[6] White, "The Historical Roots of Our Ecological Crisis."

[7] About the ecological conversion needed today, see Pope Francis's encyclical *Laudato Si'*, nos. 217–20.

[8] Nicholas Georgescu-Roegen, *The Entropy Law and the Economic Process* (Boston: Harvard University Press, 1971).

directly correlates a higher standard of living with growth of the GNP and thus maintains that a constant increase in the level of production should be a permanent goal of society. Critics raise the question of whether infinite growth is a real possibility, given that natural resources are limited. They argue that improvement in the standard of living has to be obtained without unlimited increase in consumption. Most often, these tradeoffs involve making more environmentally friendly lifestyle choices. Lester R. Brown concisely summarizes the situation by saying that "sustaining progress depends on shifting from a fossil fuel-based, automobile-centered, economy to a renewable energy-based, diversified transport, reuse/recycle economy."[9] This term—*sustaining progress*—is very similar to, and is often used interchangeably with the term *ecological living*.

Such reflections from secular society, mostly from the social sciences, posed challenges for philosophy and theology at large. Nevertheless, the Latin American approach to ecology had its own distinctive features, largely because of the determination to relate this theme to the question of the poor.

The Contribution of Leonardo Boff

The famous Brazilian theologian and thinker Leonardo Boff has continually developed a reflection upon social ecology and care for the earth. He writes:

> Social ecology doesn't have the environment as its only concern. It concerns the whole environment, inserting the human being and the society within nature. Its concerns are not only with the beauty of the city, better avenues, or squares or more attractive beaches. However, it prioritizes basic sanitary measures, a good

---

[9] Lester R. Brown, interview by Greg Ross, available on the http://www.americanscientist.org website (no date).

school network and a decent health service. Social injustice means violence against the most complex and singular being of creation: the human being, man and woman. This human being is a part and a bit of nature. Social ecology proposes a sustainable development. This is the one that responds to the basic needs of human beings today without sacrificing the natural capital of the earth, and if we consider also the needs of future generations who have a right to their satisfaction and to inherit an inhabitable earth with human relationships that are minimally just.[10]

Well being cannot simply be social; it must also be sociocosmic. That means including the cosmos within every effort to build a better life for future generations. In addition, it implies and supposes living in a sober and simple way, without excess or unnecessary luxury, while nevertheless respecting the basic desires and needs of humankind.

Boff calls on humankind to take a more critical and rational vision of the actual situation of the planet. We must act ethically in all our relationships, including our relationship with the planet, with nature, and with the "other"; we must learn to take care of the "other," to use nature in a sustainable form, taking from it only what is necessary, without abusing it, and thereby guaranteeing a future for coming generations.

---

[10] See Leonardo Boff, *Essential Care: An Ethics of Human Nature* (Waco, TX: Baylor University Press, 2008); idem, *Cry of the Earth, Cry of the Poor* (Maryknoll, NY: Orbis Books, 1997). For his reflections on the relation between Christian theology and cosmology, see Mark Hathaway and Leonardo Boff, *The Tao of Liberation: Exploring the Ecology of Transformation* (Maryknoll, NY: Orbis Books, 2009). The quotation here is translated from Leonardo Boff, "Ecologia social em face da pobreza e da exclusão," in *Ética da Vida* (Brasilia: Letraviva, 2000), 41–72.

All problems are interdependent and the problem of ecology is no exception. There is no simple solution, with one part independent of the others. Following the sad failure of negotiations of the Doha Round,[11] Leonard Boff writes:

The shameful failure of the Doha Round is due principally to the fact that the rich countries wanted an unfair share of the poor countries' markets. The opportunity to assure food on the tables of the poor was squandered, notwithstanding an environment where hunger is already widespread. The ancestral dream of human commensality, when we could all share food and communication, becomes now more distant. Apart from the food crisis, we are already suffering from the energy and climate crises. If coordinated world policies are not put in place, we face grave risks for the peoples and for the equilibrium of the planet. This is why *The Earth Charter* proposes an alliance of universal caring for the Earth by all humans, if only as a question of collective survival.

The problems are all interdependent. This is why an isolated solution with mere technical, political or commercial resources is not possible. What is needed is a coalition of new hearts and minds, imbued by universal responsibility, with values and principles of action which are indispensable for a different world order. Let's enumerate some of them:

The first of all resides in the *care* of the inheritance that we received from the immense process of the evolution of the universe.

The second is *respect* and *reverence* for all others, for each creature of nature, and for different cultures.

The third is found in the permanent *cooperation* of all with all because we are all eco-interdependent to the point of sharing a common destiny.

---

[11] The Doha Development Round, which began in 2001, is the current trade-negotiation round of the World Trade Organization. Its goal is to increase trade around the world by lowering trade barriers.

The fourth is social *justice*, one that erases differences, diminishes hierarchies and precludes inequalities.

The fifth is limitless *solidarity* and *compassion* for all beings who suffer, starting with the Earth herself, which is being crucified, and for the most vulnerable and weak.

The sixth lies in universal *responsibility* for the future of life, for the ecosystems that guarantee human survival and, in the end, for the survival of the very planet Earth herself. The seventh is *just measure* in all initiatives that are the concern of all, because we come from a cultural experience marked by excess and by inequalities.

The last is *self-control* of our voracity to accumulate and to consume, that all may have enough and that which is decent, and that all may feel that they are members of the one and only human family.

All this is only possible if, along with instrumental reason, we rescue sensible and cordial reason.

The economy cannot be independent of society, because this would destroy the very idea of society and the common good. The ideal to be sought is an economy which works for the community of life.

Politics cannot be restricted to ordain national interests, but must project a global government to equitably care for collective interests.

Spirituality must be cosmic, one that lets us "live with reverence for the mystery of being, gratitude for the gift of life, and humility regarding the human place in nature." (*The Earth Charter*, preamble)

The challenge seems to be this: to move from a society of industrial production which is at war with nature to a society that promotes all life in sync with the cycles of nature and with a sense of equity.

These are the pre-conditions of an ethical order and of a practical nature that can create an environment in which humans can get together in conviviality. Logically, certain technical, political and cultural intercessions are necessary to make this goal viable. But they will hardly be effective if they are not done in light of these guiding principles, which imply values and inspirations.[12]

Boff's insights follow the wisdom of other great figures of Christian spirituality who anticipated this vision long before the emergence of ecological awareness. I refer, for example, to Thomas Merton, the Trappist monk, who lived a spirituality deeply connected with love for creation, and the great Jesuit Pierre Teilhard de Chardin, whose mysticism was marked by the contemplation of God as the consistent dynamic force within the matter, the earth, and the world.[13] The challenge that is imposed here is to pass from a society of industrial production that is at war with nature to a society that promotes all life in harmony with natural rhythms and with a sense of equity.

Ecofeminism: A Fertile Synthesis between Ecology and Feminism

Ecofeminism is a term that was created by the French feminist Françoise d'Eaubonne in 1974 to symbolize the synthesis between environmental and ecological thinking and feminism. It is the theory that searches for an end to every form of oppression. It correlates the various dominations according to

---

[12] Leonardo Boff, "The Impossible Comensality after Doha," available on the http://www.leonardoboff.com website. This is a free translation from the Spanish by Melina Alfaro, done at Refugio Del Rio Grande, Texas.

[13] See Christine M. Bochen, ed., *Thomas Merton: Essential Writings* (Maryknoll, NY: Orbis Books, 2000); and Ursula King, ed., *Pierre Teilhard de Chardin: Essential Writing* (Maryknoll, NY: Orbis Books, 1999). See also "Teilhard de Chardin: Un mistico en comunion con el universo," *Revista Eclesiastica Brasileira –Reb* 75 (2015): 620–36; and "Thomas Merton: o amante da natureza," in *Fernando de Sousz Paiser (org) Mertonianum 100*, vol. 1 (Comemoracao do centenario de Thomas Merton (São Paulo, Brasil: Riemma Editora, 2015): 119–36.

race, gender, social class, nature, and the "other," whether women, children, the elderly, or the indigenous. Ecofeminism takes a number of forms, but they are united in the desire and struggle for a convivial society, free of domination or exploitation.

Ecofeminism in poor countries assumes a particular configuration. In countries such as those in Latin America, where many exist in a subsistence economy, the poor are the major victims of the environmental crisis. They are the first to experience deterioration in the quality of life caused by pollution or the shortage of natural resources. Ecofeminist thinking states that neither the resolution of the environmental crisis nor the oppression of women can be treated as isolated problems.

Also, according to basic ecofeminist thinking, the question of the environment is intimately related to the condition of women. This theory reflects the social division of work, as allocated within the public and private spheres. For example, in many cultures women have had the primary role of collecting food, fuel, and water for their families and communities. Therefore, women have always had a major interest in caring for nature, trying to prevent deforestation, accumulation of toxic waste, and water pollution, among other things.

Ecofeminism affirms the idea that the ecological struggle is essentially connected to women's liberation. This intimate relationship between women and nature can also be justified in terms of the process of motherhood. That is why the chosen metaphor for ecofeminism is the body: we are all part of one Sacred Body, living in a moment of revelation in which human consciousness is awakening to the sacred mysteries of the planet.[14]

Ecofeminism recognizes the connection that unites every living thing, an intuition already present among the original peoples. Ecofeminism honors the traditions of native

---

[14] See Mary Judith Ress, *Ecofeminism in Latin America* (Maryknoll, NY: Orbis Books, 2006).

cultures, which maintain a loving closeness with the earth, revered as mother and life giver. The Brazilian theologian Ivone Gebara is the major representative of Latin American ecofeminism. Gebara proposes that "an intimate articulation between a feminist line and an ecological line opens for us not only a real possibility of equality between women and men of different cultures, but also a different relationship among us, with the earth and with the whole cosmos."[15] She also affirms as a very central characteristic of ecofeminism the relationality of all beings and their fundamental interdependence, with profound implications for cosmology and anthropology.[16]

Here is her statement regarding the need for a new ethic governing our relationship to others, to nonhumans, and to the whole ecosystem: "My neighbor is myself, my sister, my brother, my neighborhood, the rivers, the seas and all the animals. Everything is my neighbor and I am neighbor of everything. Any aggression to my neighbor is an aggression to my own being. Today our challenge is to develop this ethic beyond patriarchal references, which characterized them in the past and still do so in the present."[17]

For Gebara, ecofeminism must be seen as a praxis of liberation, especially in Latin America. That is why she and those who follow her believe they must be situated within the philosophies and theologies of liberation, broadly understood. Insisting on the need to go beyond sterile discussions, Gebara calls for a search for concrete solutions to

---

[15] Ivone Gebara, *Trindade: Palavra sobre coisas velhas e novas. Uma perspectiva ecofeminista* (São Paulo: Paulinas, 1994), 158–59. See idem, *Longing for Running Water: Ecofeminism and Liberation* (Minneapolis: Fortress Press, 1999).

[16] Ivone Gebara, "Ecofeminismo: algunos desafios teológicos," *Alternativas* 16/17 (2000): 173–85. This essay answers critics who charge Latin American ecofeminism with assuming New Age aspects.

[17] Ivone Gebara, "10 años de Con-spirando," *Con-spirando* 40 (2002): 10.

daily problems; the seriousness of the situation requires immediate action. As she notes, "While all these discussions are taking place, the destruction of the rainforest continues. Hundreds of women and children are dying of hunger or of diseases provoked by a capitalist system capable of destroying lives and generating benefits only for some happy few.[18] She wants to emphasize that the destiny of the earth and the destiny of the oppressed go together. Every call for justice, therefore, implies a call for ecojustice. The oppressed in Latin American theology today include not only human beings who are poor, but also the despoiled earth, which makes the poverty of human beings even more serious.

Creation as Passion and Compassion

According to the Bible, the creative word of God is a constitutive element of the origin and ongoing activity of nature. The cosmos, in turn, is a form of God's revelation. God is the source of our existence. God calls all things into being. God's word, furthermore, creates order out of chaos. All this happens without violence, in a kind of founding sweetness that will support the development of a divine pedagogy with the chosen people. In Christian scriptures this dialogue of life and love will reach its climax in the Sermon on the Mount, wherein is proclaimed the perfection of the Father, who makes the sun to shine over the good and bad, the rain to fall over the just and unjust alike.[19]

The Bible opens with the words "in the beginning," yet there is no thought of transposing the eternity of God onto the created world. Only God is principle and beginning of everything that exists, and the world comes afterward. This

---

[18] Ibid.

[19] See Maria Clara Bingemer, "Ecologia e salvação," in *Reflexão cristã sobre o meio ambiente*, ed. Josafá Carlos de Siqueira, 30–45 (São Paulo: Loyola, 1992).

"beginning," this "origin without origin," only finds its source in the ineffable mystery that Jesus Christ called Father; it is incomprehensible and without an "end." Nevertheless, this end, without which the world would lose its dynamism, is totally unknown to us.

The recent effort put forth by Christian theology to delve into the problems of ecology and the human relationship with the totality of creation reveals a new awareness. At stake in the ecological question is much more than a new subject for reflection. What is at stake is the future of life on earth and the concept of God that is central to Christianity: God as Father and Mother, Author of life, Creator, and Savior. The effort to restore harmonious relations between humanity and the cosmos requires overcoming certain individualistic and economically deterministic concepts of the human being. It calls for us to recover a notion of life so present in the lives of ancient peoples, who saw the cosmos as epiphany, full of meaning, manifestation of mystery, a stance that called for reverence and respect.

Contemplation of the mystery of the cosmos should not be seen as an aesthetic concern born of leisure, but rather as the expression of a primary ethical concern, returning the cosmos to men and women who have been dispossessed. This restitution accompanies the struggle to give bread to the hungry, a roof to the homeless, water to the thirsty. Each of these actions entails nothing less than restoring a piece of the cosmos to those who have been deprived.

Conclusion:
The Poor as Masters and Protagonists of Ecology

Consideration of the social question of ecology must begin with the situation of the poor, in whom life itself is under the greatest threat. The poor are the major victims of the ecological disaster we are experiencing today, because they have fewer means to protect themselves.

Of course, the poor must also to take their part in the ecological struggle, and in order for this to happen, they should be adequately educated as to the issues at stake.

As the primary victims of ecological destruction, perhaps the poor can even be protagonists and masters in this field, as they have been in the midst of oppression, exemplifying and teaching principles of resilience, joy, forgiveness, and reconciliation.

As Pope Francis says in *Laudato Si'*:

> A community can break out of the indifference induced by consumerism. These actions cultivate a shared identity, with a story which can be remembered and handed on. In this way, the world, and the quality of life of the poorest, are cared for, with a sense of solidarity which is at the same time aware that we live in a common home which God has entrusted to us. (no. 232)

With this remarkable encyclical, which is being studied around the whole world, the pope reaffirms the Latin American intuition that care for the earth is inseparable from care for the poor. In other words, ecology always goes hand in hand with justice. There are two poles of the same and permanent challenge that the Creator puts to humankind every day: to struggle and take care of life, a good life, a full life for all.

5.

A Theology in Dialogue with Other Traditions

In 1492, Christopher Columbus disembarked on an island of the archipelago known today as the Bahamas, believing that he had found a new route to the land of the Indies dreamed of so fervently by Europeans. What he had discovered would come to be called America—a new continent in a time when it was naively thought the gospel had been brought and proclaimed to the whole world. This encounter inaugurated a new era of *mission*—a term previously associated with the early apostles. Now the term *mission* was applied to the heralds of the gospel in these new territories.[1]

The differences, however, were noteworthy. The first apostles had faced cruel persecution under the Roman Empire. The new apostles were chosen and sent with the complete support of "Their Most Christian and Serene Majesties," the kings of Spain and Portugal.

---

[1] See Maria Clara Luchetti Bingemer, "Contemplation and Service: Central Dynamism of Christian Mission," in *A Century of Catholic Mission: Roman Catholic Missiology 1910 to the Present*, ed. Stephen B. Bevans, 183–95 (Eugene, OR: Wipf and Stock, 2013, by arrangement with Regnum Books International).

These new apostles, protected and transported by royal power, companions of the armies that fought the "Indios," were also sustained by a powerful church, strongly hierarchical, solidly organized in terms of doctrine and discipline. It was the epoch of the Counter-Reformation, of Baroque art, of a church "triumphant over heresy." The native peoples were given a word of God that had not emptied itself, had not taken on the condition of a slave, as had the Word Incarnate (Phil 2:5–11). Some—including the Dominican friars Bartolomé de Las Casas and Antonio de Montesinos— contested this procedure, denounced abuses of power, and defended the gospel. Most of the preachers, however, lived peacefully with the enslavement they witnessed and with the practice of forced baptism. For a long time the Indios were barred from the priesthood and the episcopate. The result, even today, is the absence of an autochthonous church, especially in certain parts of the Andean region, such as in Bolivia and Peru, where indigenous populations constitute as much as 85 percent of all inhabitants. Some centuries later African slaves, especially in Brazil and Colombia, were also forced to accept the religion of the Europeans, or pretend to do so, giving their divinities the names of Catholic saints.

The church extended its presence and hegemony throughout every region, along with its strongly Latin character and emphasis on hierarchy, discipline, and doctrine. Imbued with the dogmatic mentality of the Counter-Reformation, the new apostles spread the new *Catechism of the Council of Trent* with even greater enthusiasm than they did the sacred scriptures.

Over time, the word *mission* assumed a meaning that was more juridical than theological. *Missions* became less missions of God into the world than missions from a part of the world to the rest of the planet—from Western Christendom to other latitudes. Missionaries were sent to the Turks in the East as well as to the empire of Cuzco in Peru.

Latin America: A Continent Full of Diversity

Latin America is known today as the major Christian continent in the world. Yet there is an increasing awareness of the continent's multicultural religious identity. The fact is that religion in Latin America has always been a multicultural, pluralistic phenomenon.

Thinking and speaking about God in the Southern half of the world implies returning in time to the period of colonization. When the European colonizers arrived in Latin America, they did not find a void. They found native people who worshiped gods and believed in transcendental forces.[2]

Since their first contact with people of the Caribbean and the Americas, Europeans had many different questions: anthropological, social, religious, and finally theological. Are they human? Do they have a religion? Who is their God?[3] The answers then given to these questions reflected a deep ignorance: They have no religion! or We just need to announce the gospel to them so they can be converted.[4]

---

[2] See Manuel M. Marzal, Eugenio Maurer, Xavier Albó, and Bartomeu Melià, *The Indian Face of God in Latin America* (Maryknoll, NY: Orbis Books, 1996).

[3] See José Oscar Beozzo, *O exito das telogias da libertacao e as teologias americanas contemporaneas* (São Paulo: Mimeo, 2014).

[4] Christopher Columbus writes in his diary: "I hold, most serene Princes, that if devout religious persons were here, knowing the language, they would all turn Christians" (*Journal of the First Voyage of Columbus*, American Journeys Collection, Document no. AJ-062 [Wisconsin Historical Society Digital Library and Archives, 2003], 142). For many documents relating to the conquest and evangelization of the Americas, see H. McKennie Goodpasture, ed., *Cross and Sword: An Eyewitness History of Christianity in Latin America* (Maryknoll, NY: Orbis Books, 1989); and Lee M. Penyak and Walter J. Petry, eds., *Religion in Latin America: A Documentary History* (Maryknoll, NY: Orbis Books, 2006).

As time would demonstrate, it was not as simple as that. The religious traditions of the indigenous peoples were as old, or even older in some cases, as the traditions of the colonizers, who had come in the name of the kings and queens of Portugal and Spain. It was not long before the complex realities of the clash among peoples, cultures, and religions emerged. The theological and pastoral questions posed in these origins continue to represent, even today, a burden on the conscience and the development of Latin American Christianity.

Latin America has more than three hundred indigenous peoples or ethnic groups, representing close to twenty million indigenous peoples. In Guatemala and Bolivia they constitute a majority of the population. Today, in Brazil, they number approximately one million people. Among them are diverse minority groups, spread across the country, some of which number only a few hundred members.[5] How does Christianity relate to this reality?

Two centuries after the European colonizers' conquest of our territories, the immense majority of the peoples situated at the heart of the conquered areas had accepted baptism. Exceptional missionaries, such as Dominican Bartolomé de Las Casas among the Mayas of Chiapas and Guatemala, were in some cases able to restrain military violence against the indigenous. Later, the Jesuit missions in Paraguay and elsewhere followed a similar model.[6] There were other peoples, like the Mapuches in Chile and the Guaraní in Chaco, Bolivia, who steadily resisted the conquest and evangelization until they were finally conquered by the European armies at the end of the nineteenth century.

---

[5] See René Cardozo, SJ, "Diálogo inter-religioso e povos indígenas, available in Portuguese on the http://www.cpalsj. org website.

[6] See, for instance, the film "The Mission" (1986), a historical drama about the Jesuit missions in Latin America, directed by Roland Joffé.

Even among Christianized indigenous peoples, an intense process of syncretism has prevailed in all the other aspects of their lives. Their communal life and internal form of government incorporate ancestral beliefs and practices. Expressions of their communal identity coincide frequently with religious celebrations, reflecting an appropriation of Christianity marked by their ancestral cosmovisions within a whole range of syncretisms.

For instance, in the Andes the Virgin Mary is frequently identified with Mother Earth or Pacha Mama. In addition, the work of distinguished anthropologists and theologians in Mexico has shown the elements of synthesis between the cult of the Virgin of Guadalupe and the *nahuatl* indigenous culture.[7]

The point, as these facts demonstrate, is that interreligious dialogue—whether conducted well or badly—is not a new phenomenon in Latin America; it has been a reality from the beginning. Even within an apparently solid and monolithic Catholicism, there has always been a degree of religious plurality. What is generally true in the Spanish countries of Latin America is even more so in the complex case of Brazil, which has a triple cultural matrix: Portuguese, indigenous, and African.

The Coming of the African Religions and the Difficulty of Dialogue

The confluence of the three major traditions that form the Brazilian cultural landscape has marked Brazil in quite different ways from other Latin American cultures colonized

---

[7] See Virgilio Elizondo, *Guadalupe: Mother of New Creation* (Maryknoll, NY: Orbis Books, 1997); idem, with Timothy Matovina and Allan Figueroa Deck, *The Treasure of Guadalupe* (Lanham, MD: Rowman and Littlefield Publishers, 2006). See also Ivone Gebara and Maria Clara Bingemer, *Mary: Mother of God, Mother of the Poor* (Maryknoll, NY: Orbis Books, 1989).

by Spain.[8] In Brazil, cultural and symbolic universes co-exist that are simultaneously pre-modern, modern, and post-modern.[9] This is especially true in Catholicism, which holds an important place in Brazil's religious sphere and its dialogue with other religious traditions, The religious plurality in which Brazilian Roman Catholicism grew and developed has given it an extremely rich and significant identity. The Catholic Church in Brazil has always had to confront challenges and questions that have given it a different configuration from other countries of the continent. The plurality of distinct African, indigenous, and European identities living side by side with the Roman Catholic faith has obliged Brazilian Catholics to search constantly, in a dynamic process, for their identity. This struggle has prompted Brazilian Catholics to seek new and original answers to the challenges of the times and to open spaces and paths to establish dialogue with the different religions and cultures that make up their country.

The Catholic faith was initially associated with the colonial movement of European conquest.[10] On the one hand, this resulted in the erection of barriers between the

---

[8] See Gilberto Freyre, *Casa grande e senzala* (Rio de Janeiro: Record, 1998); Sergio Buarque de Holanda, *Raízes do Brazil,* 3rd ed. (São Paulo: Companhia das Letras, 1997). We should perhaps make an exception for the Caribbean islands, which were also marked by the importation of large numbers of African slaves. But the process of cultural interaction there was different from that in Brazil.

[9] See Brazilian Bishops Conference, *Para onde vai a cultura Brasileira?* [Where is the Brazilian culture heading], especially the work of Marcelo de Carvalho Azevedo, SJ, "Dinâmicas atuais da cultura Brasileira" [Current dynamics of Brazilian culture, *Estudos da CNBB,* no. 58 (São Paulo: Paulinas, 1990), 15–47.

[10] See Heitor Frisotti, *Passos no diálogo: Igreja Católica e as religiões Afro-Brasileiras* (São Paulo: Paulus, 1996); and also the issue *Revista Humanidades: "Consciência negra"* [African consciousness] UnB, 47 (December 1999).

indigenous peoples and their traditional understanding of the sacred. On the other hand, it prompted overly hasty attempts at syncretism that were often unconscious and inconsistent,[11] with the result that "in our country the singing of the saints was not always in harmony with the dance of the orixás."[12] Over the course of four centuries, Europeans took millions of Africans from Africa. Those who survived their passage to America —no more than half—suffered a process of deculturation. Nevertheless, they continued to hold on to religious beliefs and traditions that affirmed their past. As a result, an Afro-Black-Brazilian "diaspora" culture emerged, expressed in a new family—the *família de santo* (the holy family, or religious community)—united in search of the *axé,* or vital force, which was expressed in diverse forms of religion. A similar process took place in the Caribbean Islands, Cuba, and the Antilles, with the emergence of Santería.[13]

Africans slaves were forcibly baptized into the colonizers' religion. While ostensibly accepting this new religion,

---

[11] For the concept of syncretism or mix of cultures and religions, see Afonso Soares, *Sincretismo e inculturação: Pressupostos para uma aproximação teológico-pastoral às religiões Afro-Brasileiras buscados na epistemologia de Juan Luis Segundo* (São Bernardo do Campo, Brazil: UMESP, 2001). See also *Negros, uma história de migrações* (São Paulo: Centro de Estudos Migratórios, 1996); and *Interfaces da revelação; Pressupostos para uma teologia do sincretismo religioso no Brasil* (São Paulo: Paulinas, 2003).

[12] Orixá is the name, derived from the Yoruba religion, given to the saints and divinities of Afro-Brazilian religions. See Gilbraz Aragão, "A dança dos orixás e o canto dos santos. Desafios teológico-pastorais das religiões negras do Recife" [The dance of the "orixas" and the song of the saints: The theological and pastoral challenges of Afro-Brazilian religions in Recife), doctoral thesis presented to the department of theology, Rio de Janeiro, PUC-Rio, 2002.

[13] See Orlando O. Espín, *The Faith of the People: Theological Reflections on Popular Catholicism* (Maryknoll, NY: Orbis Books, 1997).

however, they gave the names of Catholic divinities or saints to their own orixás, their manifestations of the Divine. Thus, we find in Brazilian African religions that God the Father is Oxalá, Jesus Christ is Xangô, Our Lady is Iemanjá, Saint Barbara is Iansã, Saint George is Ogum, and so on. This strategy of resistance allowed the Africans to maintain relative peaceful relationships with the white Europeans without really adopting their religion. Instead, they continued practicing their own under a Christian cover.[14]

The religious cults of African origin served as a privileged space to safeguard the cultural identity of Afro-Brazilians. Certainly, the traditional African religions retained their own cultures by reinterpreting their forms, by renaming former local gods, and by simplifying their rituals. Moreover, through this process of syncretism they were able to affirm the values of African people under new socio-historical circumstances. Hence, a new black identity was created, in configurations more or less linked to African identity. The essential feature of such configurations remained the characteristic of color, which denotes racial origin and, in the case of Brazil, a history of slavery. Cuba in 1820 and Brazil in 1888 were the last countries in Latin America to abolish slavery. As Portuguese men slept with African women, a new "mulato" (mestizo/a) population emerged as a visible sign of cultural synthesis.

Did the strategy adopted by Africans solve all of their problems? Did Afro-Brazilian and Caribbean religions find real peace and harmony in this way? Certainly not. Since the "abolition" of slavery in Brazil,[15] many persecutions were directed against the efforts of *terreiros*,[16] those of African

---

[14] See Geraldo Jose da Rocha *Teologia e Negritude* (São Paulo: Paulinas, 1999).

[15] Brazilian liberationist groups question the statement that slavery was actually abolished in Brazil in 1888. Slavery, as they understand it, continues to exist.

[16] *Terreiro* is the place of worship and liturgy of the Afro-Brazilian religions.

descent who tried to resume their religious practices. These persecutions were obviously connected to the racial question. Today, people of African descent make up a large part of the Brazilian population. However, they belong mostly to the poor classes of society and find obstacles almost everywhere: to get jobs, to be accepted socially, and to enjoy the opportunities available to those of European descent.[17] In spite of this, their religious ceremonies are sought out by white people who enjoy the experience of the dance and the music of the Candomblé. And Carnival, a festival first appropriated by African descendants, has become a commercialized event, attracting multitudes of tourists.

As we can see, in the case of the indigenous and African descendants, the problem or difference in culture and religious tradition is deeply connected to the problem of poverty, a connection of increasing interest to liberation theology.

The Difficulties of Religious Pluralism and Liberation Theology

Although it is impossible to deny the importance of the "other" in liberation theology, this focus has tended to concentrate on the figure of the poor, the oppressed, and the exploited classes. In the first decades since the emergence of liberation theology there was little concern with opening to other religious traditions.

Even among liberation theologians who concerned themselves with the subject of popular religion, there was little impulse to engage with the rich and diverse religious cul-

---

[17] See Franco Cagnasso et al., *Desafios da missão* (São Paulo: Mundo e Missão, 1995); Paulo Suess. *Evangelizar a partir dos projetos históricos dos outros—Ensaio de missiologia* (São Paulo: Paulus, 1995); Agenor Brighenti, *Por uma evangelização inculturada: Princípios pedagógicos e passos metodológicos* (São Paulo: Paulinas, 1998).

ture of the continent. Even in the case of popular religion, the approach of certain liberation theologians has been ambivalent, tending sometimes to contrast popular religion or religiosity with liberating faith. There are many examples of this tendency in the works of the pioneers of liberation theology.[18] A similar tendency occurs in liberation theology's concern with "purifying" popular religiosity from its "alienating" and "oppressing" elements.[19] We can see this tendency also in documents of the Latin American Episcopate, for instance in the 1979 Puebla document:

> Due to the lack of attention on the part of pastoral agents and other complicated factors, the religion of the people shows signs of erosion and distortion. Aberrant substitutes and regressive forms of syncretism have already surfaced. (no. 453)[20]

With the crisis of 1989, liberation theology began to enlarge its scope, paying attention to other topics, such as gender, race, ethnicity, and ecology. Nevertheless, the theology of religious pluralism, which had already begun in the First World,[21] didn't initially capture the interest Latin

---

[18] Aloysius Pieris, a Sri Lankan Jesuit, examines this question in *An Asian Theology of Liberation* (Maryknoll, NY: Orbis Books, 1988).

[19] João Batista Libanio, *Teologia da libertação: Roteiro didático para um estudo* (São Paulo: Loyola, 1987), 279. For an analysis of the evolving attitude of liberation theology toward "popular religion," see Harvey Cox, "Seven Samurai and How They Looked Again: Theology, Social Analysis, and Religión Popular in Latin America," in *The Future of Liberation Theology: Essays in Honor of Gustavo Gutiérrez*, ed. Marc H. Ellis and Otto Maduro, 229–39 (Maryknoll, NY: Orbis Books, 1989).

[20] For an English translation of the final document, see John Eagleson and Philip Scharper, eds., *Puebla and Beyond* (Maryknoll, NY: Orbis Books, 1979).

[21] See Paul Knitter, *Introducing Theologies of Religion* (Maryknoll, NY: Orbis Books, 2002).

American theologians. It was treated as an academic subject restricted to European theology. It is a fact that in Latin America the majority of people are "officially" Catholic. Liberation theology initially appeared in groups dedicated to renewing the mission of the church in service to people within strongly Catholic cultures. Even interest in ecumenism was not strong in Latin America until the 1990s,[22] when a more visible collaboration emerged between Catholics and Protestants in organizations such as the base ecclesial communities; women's groups; Bible circles; and pastoral projects around the land, the Indigenous, and so on. This was a practical ecumenism rather than an effective ecumenical ecclesiology elaborated in academic or theological circles.

Starting in the mid-1990s, there began to emerge in many circles of pastoral and liberation theology a greater concern about the inculturation of faith and Christian language. It was becoming clear that Christian pastoral work was impossible without entering the culture of the "other."[23]

In brief, as has been noted, in order to ensure their cultural survival, oppressed peoples of African descent entered into dialogue with the religion of the colonizers and with the religions of other people, such as indigenous religions. They forged a synthesis between Christianity and the African-based cults and rituals, such as the Candomblé in Bahia, the Xangô in Recife, the Santería in Cuba and the Dominican

---

[22] We cannot forget important works with ecumenism since the first hour. See, for example, José Míguez Bonino, *Faces of Latin American Protestantism: 1993 Carnahan Lectures* (Grand Rapids, MI: Eerdmans, 1997); idem, *Faces of Jesus: Latin American Christologies* (Maryknoll, NY: Orbis Books, 1984); Rubem Alves, *A Theology of Human Hope* (St. Meinrad, IN: Abbey Press: 1974); Julio de Santa Ana, *Toward a Church of the Poor* (Maryknoll, NY: Orbis Books, 1980); and Guillermo Cook, *New Face of the Church in Latin America* (Maryknoll, NY: Orbis Books, 1994).

[23] See Diego Irrarázaval, *Inculturation: A New Dawn of the Church in Latin America* (Maryknoll, NY: Orbis Books, 2000).

Republic, and the Afro cults in Colombia. Speaking about the synthesis of the native peoples on the continent, Eliezer Lopes, a Mexican Zapoteco theologian, affirms: [The people knew how] "to reformulate their culture . . . in the context of the system. . . . They re-read the Christian religion to give continuity within it to the ancestral religious traditions of our peoples."[24] Diego Irarrázaval adds and explains:

> In accordance with the features of each region and according to local processes, people have developed in their own spaces and times. . . . This plurality of spaces and of moments of salvific well-being entails a range of religious functions and types of leadership. We also have a number of ways of invoking and understanding the sacred. It looks like a form of polytheism, but actually it is a human polycentrism with its religious reference points.[25]

In addition, the attention of liberation theology shifted to popular religion through the insertion of religious communities in the world of the poor. At first the preferential option for the poor relied on a lens that understood poverty from a socio-economical-political perspective. However, another side of this inculturation began to emerge as pastoral agents inserted in the world of the poor began to identify more with the religious culture of the people. For instance, in the diocese of São Felix do Araguaia, in Brazil, a fraternity of the Little Sisters of Jesus lived in a village of the Tapirapé, an indigenous tribe. They identified themselves with the people there. Sister Genoveva, a French nun, who recently died, was recognized by the indigenous community as a true Tapirapé. During the 1970s, Bartholomé Meliá, SJ, a Spanish priest who lived with the indigenous Salumã in

---

[24] Eleazar Lopes, cited in ibid., 78.
[25] Irrarázaval, *Inculturation*, 77.

Paraguay, also took part in their religious rituals. And Fr. François de l'Espinay, a Frenchman who was very committed to liberation theology, became a member of a community of Candomblé, in Bahia.[26]

These were decisive movements in the development of a spirituality of liberation. With the practice of this spirituality a whole movement of openness and diversity emerged. The concept of "macro ecumenism" grew stronger, with a new consciousness of an ecumenism sealed by the universality of the people of God, an understanding that the people of God consist of many peoples.[27]

In the year 2000, Peruvian theologian Gustavo Gutiérrez, presenting the new Brazilian edition of his theology of liberation, wrote a long preface in which he showed how this theology has enlarged its perspective. He underlined particularly the importance of the dialogue established with other theologies (Asian and African), thus contributing to better understanding and appreciation of the poor and aspects of their culture. Gutiérrez pointed to the fact of religious pluralism and the emergence of interreligious dialogue as among the most fundamental challenges of our time[28]

---

[26] François De L'Espinay, "Igreja e Religião Africana do Candomblé no Brasil, in *Revista Eclesiástica Brasileira* 47 (December 1987): 870.

[27] See Faustino Teixeira, *O diálogo inter-religioso como afirmação da vida* (São Paulo: Paulinas, 1997), 150; and Pedro Cadaldáliga and José María Vigil, *Political Holiness: A Spiritiuality of Liberation* (Maryknoll, NY: Orbis Books, 1994).

[28] Gustavo Gutiérrez, "Situação e tarefas da teologia da libertação," in *Sarça ardente*, ed. Luiz Carlos Susin (São Paulo: Paulinas/SOTER, 2000), 55–57. To Gutiérrez, theology will have to pay careful attention to this theme, understanding it as a sign of the times, searching to discern, "in the light of faith, the new hermeneutical field being proportioned in order to think about Faith and to speak about God in a way that speaks to people of our time" (52).

From Separation, through Dialogue, to Double (Multiple) Belonging

At this point a question emerges: Is it possible for a person who belongs to one particular socio-religious group to feel at home and participate in another? That is, can two or more religions or spiritual traditions coexist within one single individual? At an abstract level, either sociologically or philosophically, the answer would probably be, no. Each religion considers its view of the world and its doctrines to be absolute truths. It seems unthinkable that someone would be able to believe in two different systems of truth at the same time. However, when we analyze the situation in phenomenological terms, we meet people who seem to feel at home in two different religious traditions. Outsiders regard these as syncretistic or parallel religious systems, but their practitioners seem comfortable with both.

Many contemporary theologians see a combination and even an integration of local cosmic religiosities as something that is not only normal but even inevitable and necessary.[29] These phenomena can be found all over the world where the so-called great religions spread across new geographical areas. The cosmic and meta-cosmic nature of the different elements within them does not make their coexistence or even their integration a problem. People actually live in different symbolic worlds and seem to move from one to the other with ease. Coexistence, if not integration, between the two is often marked by local historical and social conditions. Various studies of popular religiosity in different continents have shown that, alongside the official and approved liturgies of the churches, people continue to invoke other powers—often spirits and ancestors—in times of need for protection

---

[29] See Catherine Cornille, *Many Mansions? Multiple Religious Belonging and Christian Identity* (Maryknoll, NY: Orbis Book, 2002); Paul Knitter and Roger Haight, *Jesus and Buddha; Friends in Conversation* (Maryknoll, NY: Orbis Books, 2015).

from danger; for healing from physical, mental, and social diseases; and for establishing favorable relations with the powers of nature and society. Such rituals are prevalent in rites of passage in individual and social life. These practices in the form of popular devotions are variously condemned, tolerated, or even encouraged by the official church. Sacred places and times, powerful mediators, living or dead, pilgrimages, and special penances are common all over the world, even today.[30] Moreover, that seems to be the case in Latin America with indigenous and African traditions.

Therefore, is it possible to drink from more than one well, to live several faiths, to follow several guides? If the answer is yes, under what conditions? Taking a closer look, it seems that a "double belonging" does not mean that someone lives fully within two traditions in a parallel way and at the same level. Is it not more fruitful to understand this phenomenon as a dynamic and spiritual movement in which one is exposed to another tradition and embraces it without leaving behind one's own? In such an encounter, beyond surface curiosity, there runs the acknowledgment of a need and a thirst that the pilgrim—the one who passes from one religious belonging to another—cannot ignore.[31]

Today, an important trend within Christian theology has developed the conviction that every religion, within its own limits, bears seeds of truth and is a bearer of a form of genuine salvation.[32] It becomes increasingly evident that

---

[30] See Cornille, *Many Mansions?* See also Hans Küng et al., *Christianity and World Religions: Paths to Dialogue* (Maryknoll, NY: Orbis Books, 1993).

[31] For the concept of religion as place of transit, see Michel de Certeau, *La faiblesse de croire* (Paris: Cerf, 1989).

[32] See, first of all, *Nostra aetate* of the Second Vatican Council. Among post-conciliar theologies, see, among others, Jacques Dupuis, *Toward a Christian Theology of Religious Pluralism* (Maryknoll, NY: Orbis Books, 1994); and Michael Amaladoss, *Making All Things New: Dialogue, Pluralism, and Evangelization in Asia* (Maryknoll, NY: Orbis Books, 1990).

the encounters among religions must not occur in a context of mutual accusation or threats but in an atmosphere of respect and dialogue. Therefore, relations between Christianity and African-Brazilian religious traditions would not have to deny each other's truth or salvation. On the contrary, they might find mutual renewal and enrichment.

Conclusion

Liberation theologians have engaged in dialogue with many theologians from Asia and elsewhere. This dialogue has borne much fruit. For instance, the new generation of Indian theologians (such as Jesuits Aloysius Pieris and Michael Amaladoss) have eagerly incorporated many insights from liberation theology. These theologians welcomed, with great interest, the new models of theological thinking and pastoral praxis that came from Latin America, which they integrated with the pressing Asian challenge of religious pluralism. Other theologians have also seen the urgency in fostering greater interaction between liberation theology and theology of religions. As Paul Knitter writes:

> The liberation theologians are realizing that economic, political, and especially nuclear liberation is too big a job for any one nation, or culture, or religion. A cross-cultural interreligious sharing of liberation theory and praxis is needed. And theologians of religions are recognizing that a dialogue among religions that does not promote the welfare of all humanity is not a religious dialogue.[33]

---

[33] Paul Knitter, "Catholic Theology at a Crossroads," *Concilium* 203/1 (1986), 111. See also idem, *Jesus and the Other Names: Christian Mission and Global Responsibility* (Maryknoll, NY: Orbis Books, 1996).

We can also remember Hans Küng, who in the early 1990s initiated a project called the Global Ethics Foundation, an attempt to describe what the world's religions have in common rather than what separates them, and to draw up a minimal code of ethical rules that everyone can accept. His vision of a global ethic was embodied in the document for which he wrote the initial draft, *Toward a Global Ethic: An Initial Declaration.* This declaration was signed at the 1993 Parliament of the World's Religions by religious and spiritual leaders from around the globe. Later, Küng's project would culminate in the UN's *Dialogue among Civilizations,* to which Küng was assigned as one of nineteen "eminent persons."

All of this bears a double challenge. On the one hand, there is the importance of enlarging the regional limitations of liberation theology and expanding its openness to other religions; on the other hand, there is the important challenge to theologies of religion to embrace the option for the impoverished and excluded, taking seriously the issues of poverty and oppression.[34] The singularity and richness animating these two theologies is undeniable. They are creative and revitalizing expressions for contemporary theological

---

[34] As Paul Knitter has observed, just as liberation theology couldn't relativize attention given to the global cultural and religious context, theology of religions also has to be attentive to the common and human experience of suffering as a "new 'hermeneutical kairos' for interreligious encounter" ("Christian Theology of Liberation and Interfaith Dialogue," in *Christianity and Other Religions,* ed. John Hick and Brian Hebblethwaite (London: Oneworld Publications, 2001). See also Paul Knitter, *One Earth, Many Religions: Multifaith Dialogue and Global Responsibility* (Maryknoll, NY: Orbis Books, 1995); and his essay "Toward a Liberation Theology of Religions," in *The Myth of Christian Uniqueness: Toward a Pluralistic Theology of Religions,* ed. John Hick and Paul Knitter, 178–200 (Maryknoll, NY: Orbis Books, 1987).

thought. Moreover, they try to address a provocative issue that challenges the churches and religions today: the painful reality of injustice along with the richness of plurality and diversity among religions and cultures.

Perhaps the deepest convergence that links liberation theology with the Christian theology of religions is the same passion for the larger horizon that we Christians call the salvation of the kingdom of God. More than an institutional belonging and reference, these two theologies are interested in building a better life for everyone and everything.

In that light, the challenge is to form interreligious symbology of the kingdom of God, a mystery that implies a deep relation among all religions without being strictly confined to any one of them. Achieving this goal means welcoming the value of otherness, recognizing in each tradition a source of infinite mystery, with a deep and true meaning that can't be fully translated. Thus, each singularity and each religious tradition is preserved.

This common passion for salvation and for the kingdom of God becomes an exercise in promoting compassion, seeking life, and affirming justice for all. Johann Baptist Metz calls this compassionate searching the heart of theological identity: "The discourse about God can only be universal, or significant for all human beings, if in its center it translates a discourse about a God sensitive to the suffering of others."[35]

David Tracy has noted that many mystical experiences begin with the awareness of suffering or with attention to other's suffering.[36] Let us hope that the desire to heal and to alleviate human suffering will become a path for religions to engage in dialogue and come closer to building a world of peace and justice for everyone.

---

[35] Johann B. Metz, "La compasión. Un programa universal del cristianismo en la época de pluralismo cultural y religioso," *Revista Latinoamericana de Teología* 19/55 (January-April 2002): 27.

[36] "Afterword: A Reflection on Mystics: Presence and Aporia," in *Mysticis: Presence and Aporia,* ed. Michael Kessler and Christian Sheppard, 239–44 (Chicago: University of Chicago Press, 2003).

Conclusion

The Future of
Latin American Theology

It has been important to revisit the past, to understand the roots and the origins of Latin American theology, so that we might continue to think theologically at the service of our peoples as we move forward.

As Jon Sobrino says, there are pasts that kill and bury ideals and dreams. In addition, there are pasts that have the power to launch transformative and life-giving processes.[1] The Latin American church has a very blessed and shining past. It is a church that built something new in Christian history, contributing to the wider church perhaps the most original and valuable reception and interpretation of Vatican II.

This glorious past, which includes a fertile and abundant body of theological work, and which is sealed by the witness of many martyrs and confessors, continues to enlighten and inspire those who desire to build a different world. Therefore, this memory is and will always be a subversive memory that no power and no oppressor will erase.

---

[1] Jon Sobrino, *The Principle of Mercy: Taking the Crucified People from the Cross* (Maryknoll, NY: Orbis Books, 1994).

Not only has Latin American theology left its impact on the social doctrine of the church, but it has exercised an influence on countless people, among them Pope Francis, Because of this theology, the victims of history are not forgotten and the poor are not excluded from theological attention; on the contrary, they are present, inspiring and moving theological efforts today.

Apart from this, we have seen that this past, when faced with critical attention, was capable of generating a new present. Moreover, this present was not sterile and uncreative; rather, it was alive and dynamic. We have seen how, despite the difficult moments in the 1980s and 1990s, Latin American theology was not defeated; on the contrary, it expanded its scope, incorporating new themes into its research and reflection. Moreover, Latin American theologians remained faithful to their essential position: the preferential option for the poor. They found new and creative ways to live this out.

As a part of this creativity we have seen the theology of the continent turning its sight toward other—anthropological—poverties, such as those related to ecology, gender, and interreligious dialogue. It did so in such a fashion as to remain always connected with the central Latin American positions: liberation from all kinds of oppression and struggle against exclusion, against discriminations of every configuration (race, sex, ethnicity, and so forth), and against all forms of domination and prejudice. And, most of all, it expressed a deep love: a compassionate love for all the victims and all those who keep hope alive.

Increasingly, Latin American theology identifies its locus in everyday life,[2] the resistance of those who cling to life when there are countless reasons to give up and die. The

---

[2] See Ada-Maria Isasi Días, "*Lo Cotidiano*: Everyday Struggles in Hispanas/Latinas' Lives," in *La Lucha Continues: Mujerista Theology* 92–106 (Maryknoll, NY: Orbis Books, 2004), 95. See also Enrique Dussel, Jorge Pixley, and Pablo Richard, eds., *Contextos y Balances de la Teologia De La Liberacion* (Quito, Ecuador: Ediciones Abya-Ayala, 1998).

revolutionary potential of these everyday practices should not be easily dismissed. To quote Marc Bloch, great rebellions are "mere flashes in the pan." They are "almost invariably doomed to defeat and eventual massacre." Nevertheless, "the patient, silent struggles stubbornly carried on by the rural communities over the years would accomplish more than these flashes in the pan."[3] I would modify that by saying not only rural communities, but all poor communities—rural, urban, and migrant. In the face of totalitarian power, dominated peoples demonstrate their own resilience, reacting to the dominant powers in ingenious ways so as to contribute to their well being and that of the "other."

For this reason Latin American theology should persist in utilizing the method that has been consecrated for many decades in developing its theological reflection: see-judge-act. To see reality, to evaluate it critically, to feel challenged by its facts and dangers as well as its beauties and glories—this is the essential foundation so that Latin American theology may preserve its freedom and sustain its momentum. To abandon this direction is to be coopted by the rigid logic of dominant social (and ecclesiastical) power.

Another important point to be treated carefully when we think about the future of Latin American theology is undoubtedly the question of conflict and violence. This is not new in our continent, and liberation theology has devoted much attention to this subject.[4] Violence is far from being overcome on the continent. However, its face has changed. Now, instead of the army and the soldiers, many times coming from elsewhere, the agents of violence are often the drug traffickers inside the countries and youth gangs.

Latin America is a crucial geographic zone for drug production and trafficking. The Andean countries of Colombia,

---

[3] Marc Bloch, *French Rural History: An Essay on Its Basic Characteristics*, trans. Janet Sondheimer (Berkeley and Los Angeles: University of California Press, 1970), 170.

[4] Jon Sobrino and Ignacio Ellacuría, for example, have considered the subject of military violence in El Salvador; see also the homilies of Oscar Romero.

Peru, and Bolivia are the world's main producers of cocaine, while Central America, Mexico, and the Caribbean have become the principal corridors for transporting drugs into the United States and Europe. In Brazil, slums and poor neighborhoods surround the big cities where children and youngsters are coopted by the traffickers to carry out the transportation of drugs. A whole generation of young men is steadily falling victim to violence every year. In 2014 "Brazil reached a new peak of violence . . . with more than 58,000 violent deaths,"[5] approximately the total number of Americans killed during the Vietnam War.

The countries of the region have suffered various consequences of drug trafficking, including forms of both environmental and community damage. The guerrilla insurgent groups are an example: the FARC in Colombia and the Shining Path (Sendero Luminoso) in Peru. Throughout the entire region, in both drug production and trafficking areas, there has been an upsurge in violence, corruption, impunity, erosion of the rule of law, and human rights violations caused by the emergence of powerful organized crime rings and drug cartels.

On the other hand, the whole world is suffering—as Pope Francis often describes it—a form of piecemeal third-world war. Radical jihadist groups in the Middle East are making entire cities disappear, and their violence is spreading around the globe. Children suffer violence, as do women and the elderly, along with men. Panic dominates the region and forces many people, even more than before, to flee to the richer countries of North America and Europe. Christian theology and ethics must speak to these challenges. Faithful to reality, we must revisit the gospel, searching out new and creative paths toward facing the big question of migration and trying to make peace a concrete reality in our world.

---

[5] "Violent Deaths in Brazil Surge to Peak of 58,000 amid Olympic Safety Fears," Reuters, *The Guardian* (US edition) (October 8, 2015).

The challenge for Latin American theology is to persevere in accomplishing the priorities it has set over the past fifty years. This requires that we rescue the memory and testimony of those who built these priorities and worked on them even at the risk of their own security and lives. More than ever we need a theology of witnesses, of spiritual masters, more than erudite and abstract texts. In this sense the biographies of the mystics, the martyrs, and the saints are powerful "living texts" that we can revisit and whose reserves of light and wisdom will never be exhausted.[6] Latin American theology is born from the vital experience and the sacrifice of a cloud of witnesses, men and women who devoted themselves to making possible a different future for the continent. Today, this task is ours, and we must present it to the new generations as a challenge worth all their creativity, imagination, and sacrifice.

---

[6] See, for example, Jon Sobrino, *Witnesses to the Kingdom: The Martyrs of El Salvador and the Crucified Peoples* (Maryknoll, NY: Orbis Books, 2003). See also the many books about the witness of Oscar Romero, including María López Vigil, *Monseñor Romero: Memories in Mosaic* (Maryknoll, NY: Orbis Books, 2013). See also Maria Clara Bingemer and Peter Casarella, eds., *Witnessing Prophecy, Politics, and Wisdom* (Maryknoll, NY: Orbis Books, 2014).

Index